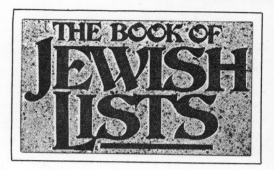

THE BOOK OF JEWISH LISTS

"Entertaining, informative, and impressive"
— The Detroit Jewish News

More than one hundred thirty fascinating lists about Jews and things Jewish, including:

* Independent Jewish Kingdoms Outside Israel
* The World's Most Important Jews
* Peoples Who May Be the Lost Ten Tribes
* Jews Hailed as the Messiah
* Jewish Crewmembers of the Starship *Enterprise*
* Relationships Held Incestuous by Jewish Law
* Jews on the Faculty of Harvard
* Jewish Vegetarians
* Sects of Black Hebrews
* Female Jewish Religious Scholars
* Famous Shabbos Goyim
* Jewish Professional Wrestlers
* Short Jewish Baseball Stories
* Great Jewish Psychotherapists
* Menachem Begin's List of Most Inspiring Religious Figures
* and many, many more!

Many of these authoritative lists place the emphasis on the offbeat and humorous. Imaginatively chosen for the Chosen, they're as much fun to browse as to read straight through. Here's a book that's a perfect gift for others—and to give yourself.

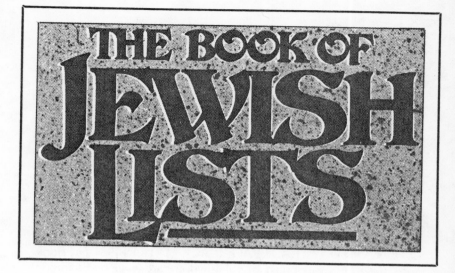

THE BOOK OF JEWISH LISTS

REVISED AND UPDATED

RON LANDAU

STEIN AND DAY/*Publishers*/New York

STEIN AND DAY TRADE PAPERBACK EDITION 1984 *The Book of Jewish Lists* was originally published in hardcover by Stein and Day/*Publishers* in 1982 and has been updated for this paperback edition.

Designed by Judith E. Dalzell
Printed in the United States of America
STEIN AND DAY /*Publishers*
Scarborough House
Briarcliff Manor, N.Y. 10510

Library of Congress Cataloging in Publication Data

Landau, Ron.
   The book of Jewish lists.

   Includes index.
      1.   Jews—Miscellanea.   I.   Title.
DS118.5.L34   909'.04924   83-40354
ISBN 0-8128-6214-7   AACR2

CONTENTS

SOURCES AND ACKNOWLEDGMENTS

I wish to thank my many friends who provided me with a steady flow of information and sound advice, especially Mr. and Mrs. Craig Karpel. Special thanks are due to the many well-known personalities who were kind enough to provide me with their lists. Above all, I want to thank my wife, Pearl, whose hard work and good judgment were essential to the compilation of this book.

Literally hundreds of books and thousands of magazines and journals were consulted in the compilation of this volume. To mention all of them would make for a very long and boring list indeed. Let it suffice to say that the three sources I drew upon more than any others were the *Jewish Digest,* the *Jewish Post and Opinion,* and the *Jewish Press.* Sources have not been cited in the text except in a few of the more incredible entries.

ACKNOWLEDGMENTS TO THE SECOND EDITION

I would like to thank the following for bringing to my attention errors in the first edition: Alazar Templeton, Neal A. Filler, Neal Sturman, Mrs. Ruffy Silverstein, Gerald Silverman, Bridget Goldschmidt, Leonard Simons, Mrs. Victor Trager, Michael Posner, David Rudolph, Jerry Greenstein, and Joseph Oppenheimer.

I thank the following for new information that appears in this edition: Rose Collova, Tommy Carpenshtella, Gershon Leebhoff, and Hosea Greenfield.

INTRODUCTION

Some 1800 years ago, the rabbis who wrote the Talmud explained their educational methodology: "Make mnemonics for the Torah," they advised. The ancient rabbinic literature is full of mnemonic devices, especially lists. But even those sages were not really innovators; in this respect, they probably took their cue from the oldest of Jewish books, the Bible itself. Besides containing the most famous list of all time, the Ten Commandments, other large sections of the Bible are presented in list form.

The idea of an entire book of lists is also a Jewish invention. No, I'm not referring to the Wallechinsky-Wallaces, who, of course, are Jewish. The first book of lists was compiled by Noah Haim, a nineteenth-century Polish Jew, who collected most of the lists found in Jewish literature up to his day.

The nature of the appeal that lists have for the reader—and the writer—can be summed up in one word: clarity. No other form presents sundry bits of related information to the reader in a manner more suitable for memorization and comparison. The result—providing that subject matter is interesting enough—is a feeling of immediate satisfaction, getting right to the point, tackling the information and mastering it. It is undoubtedly for this reason that lists have been a traditional Jewish literary device and a popular one to this day.

The theme that has guided my selection of material for this book is a line from that medieval classic *The Kuzari,* "As the heart is to the limbs, so are the Jews to the other nations." Just as the Jews have been the most creative people to inhabit this planet, so, too, have they been the most vibrant and colorful. This book is an attempt to capture some of that color, not without a touch of pride. Martin Greenberg, in his *The Jewish Lists,* has compiled a fine compendium of Jewish accomplishments. While not neglecting that area, the accent in this is more on the unique, the offbeat, and the humorous. Though *The Book of Jewish Lists* does have considerable value as a reference book, it has been my aim throughout simply to provide enjoyable reading. I hope you will decide that I have succeeded.

Just a few final words on the question of who is a Jew. Wherever the information was available, I followed the traditional formula of considering anyone born to a Jewish mother Jewish. I also have included converts to Judaism even where their conversions did not meet Orthodox rabbinic standards. My identification of people as Jewish is only as accurate as my sources, however. In a few instances, I've relied upon obviously Jewish-sounding names. As I know personally very few of the people listed in this book it is possible that some errors have crept in. Still, I hope that those few non-Jews inadvertently included will feel honored to be chosen with the Chosen.

1.
Would You Believe?

ONE HUNDRED FIFTY-NINE JEWS AND THE NAMES UNDER WHICH THEY BECAME FAMOUS

1. Frank Abelson—FRANKIE VAUGHAN (British singer)
2. Joseph Abramowitz—JOEY ADAMS (comedian)
3. Hyman Arluck—HAROLD ARLEN (composer of "Over the Rainbow")
4. Abraham Isaac Arshawsky—ARTIE SHAW (swing bandleader)
5. Israel Baline—IRVING BERLIN (composer)
6. Judah Bergman—JACKIE BERG (world welterweight boxing champion, 1930–31)
7. Rosine Bernard—SARAH BERNHARDT (French actress)
8. Milton Berlinger—MILTON BERLE (comedian)
9. Nathan Birnbaum—GEORGE BURNS (comedian, actor)
10. Marcel Bloch—MARCEL DASSAULT (French aircraft industry baron)
11. Rosebud Blustein—JOAN BLONDELL (actress)
12. Abraham Borowitz—ABE BURROWS (playwright)

13. Lev Davidovich Bronstein—LEON TROTSKY (Russian Communist leader)
14. Louis Buchalter—LOUIS LEPKE (gangster)
15. Charles Buchinsky—CHARLES BRONSON (actor)
16. Albert Caplin—AL CAPP (creator of Li'l Abner)
17. Jack Chakrin—JACK CARTER (comedian)
18. Aaron Chwatt—RED BUTTONS (comedian)
19. Berl Cohen—BÉLA KUN (head of Hungary's short-lived 1919 Communist government)
20. Howard Cohen—HOWARD COSELL (sportscaster)
21. Jacob Cohen—RODNEY DANGERFIELD (comedian)
22. Shmuel Yosef Czaczkes—S. Y. AGNON (Nobel Prize-winning novelist)
23. Isser Danielovitch Demsky—KIRK DOUGLAS (film star)
24. David Dobnievski—DAVID DUBINSKY (American labor leader)
25. Morton Dubnitsky—MORTON DEAN (CBS news correspondent)
26. Albert Einstein—ALBERT BROOKS (comedian)
27. Walter Ericson—HOWARD FAST (novelist)
28. Isador Feinstein—I. F. STONE (journalist, author)
29. Philip Feldman—PHIL FOSTER (Papa in TV's "Laverne and Shirley")
30. Sophie Feldman—TOTIE FIELDS (comedienne)
31. Larry Fineberg—LARRY FINE (Larry of the Three Stooges)
32. Arnold Lawrence Finkelstein—ARNIE LAWRENCE (jazz musician)
33. Jacob Finkelstein—JACKIE FIELDS (world welterweight boxing champion, 1929–30, '32, '33)
34. Mark Finkelstein—MARK HARRIS (novelist)
35. Harve Fischman—HARVE BENNETT (TV producer)

36. Arthur Flegenheimer—DUTCH SCHULTZ (gangster)
37. Esther Pauline Friedman—ANN LANDERS (advice columnist)
38. Pauline Esther Friedman—ABIGAIL VAN BUREN (advice columnist, Ann Landers's twin sister)
39. Theodore Leopold Friedman—TED LEWIS (star of jazz, vaudeville, and films)
40. Andrei Friedman—ROBERT CAPA (war photographer)
41. Julius Garfinkle—JOHN GARFIELD (early film star)
42. Jack Gellman—JACK GILFORD (comedian)
43. Richard Ginsberg—RICHARD GOODWIN (speechwriter for Pres. Lyndon Johnson)
44. Burton Mitchell Goldberg—B. MITCHELL REED (once LA's top disc jockey)
45. Emanuel Goldberg—EDWARD G. ROBINSON (TV and film star)
46. Aaron Hirsh Goldbogen—MICHAEL TODD (film producer)
47. Samuel Goldfish—SAMUEL GOLDWYN (founder of Metro-Goldwyn-Mayer
48. Herschel Goldhirsch—HARRY GOLDEN (author, journalist)
49. Henryk Goldszmidt—JANUSZ KORCZAK (Warsaw ghetto hero)
50. Theodosia Goodman—THEDA BARA (early film star)
51. Ira Gossel—JEFF CHANDLER (film star)
52. Joseph Abraham Gottlieb—JOEY BISHOP (comedian)
53. Irwin Granich—MICHAEL GOLD (novelist)
54. David Green—DAVID BEN GURION (Israili Prime Minister)
55. Shmuel Greenberg—SHECKY GREENE (comedian)
56. Leonard Hacker—BUDDY HACKETT (comedian)

57. Monty Halparin—MONTY HALL (TV personality)
58. Emile Herzog—ANDRE MAUROIS (French novelist)
59. Melvyn Hesselberg—MELVYN DOUGLAS (film star)
60. Moshe Hillkowitz—MORRIS HILLQUIT (early U.S. socialist leader)
61. Jacob Horowitz—JED HARRIS (Broadway producer)
62. Jerome Horowitz—CURLY HOWARD (Curly of the Three Stooges)
63. Maurice Horowitz—MOE HOWARD (Moe of the Three Stooges)
64. Samuel Horowitz—SHEMP HOWARD (Shemp of the Three Stooges)
65. Melvin Israel—MEL ALLEN (baseball announcer)
66. Edward Isadore Itskowitz—EDDIE CANTOR (singer)
67. Leo Jacob—LEE J. COBB (film star)
68. Bert Jacobson—BERT PARKS (MC for the Miss America Pageant, 1956–1979)
69. Paul Jacobson—PAUL MARC (actor)
70. Murray Janofsky—JAN MURRAY (comedian)
71. Israel Beer Josaphat—PAUL JULIUS von REUTER (founder of Reuter's News Agency)
72. Romain Kacev—ROMAIN GARY (novelist)
73. Sonia Kalish—SOPHIE TUCKER (singer)
74. Simone Kaminker—SIMON SIGNORET (film star)
75. Daniel Kaminsky—DANNY KAYE (comedian)
76. Melvin Kaminsky—MEL BROOKS (comedian, film director)
77. Ephraim Katchalski—EPHRAIM KATZIR (President of Israel)
78. Joel Katz—JOEL GREY (film star)
79. Seymour Kaufman—CY COLEMAN (composer of "Hey,

Look Me Over," "Big Spender," and many more popular tunes)

80. Sandor Kellner—SIR ALEXANDER KORDA (film producer)
81. Irwin Allen Kinberg—ALAN KING (comedian)
82. Ferenc Kisont—EFRAIM KISHON (Israeli humorist)
83. Eugene Klass—GENE BARRY (actor)
84. Barbara Klein—BARBI BENTON (*Playboy* model, singer)
85. Carol Klein—CAROLE KING (pop singer, songwriter)
86. Judith Klein—JUDITH CRIST (film and drama critic)
87. John Kline—JOHNNY KLING (early baseball star with the Chicago Cubs)
88. Allan Stewart Koenigsberg—WOODY ALLEN (humorist, film star)
89. Jacob Krantz—RICARDO CORTEZ (early film star)
90. Benny Kubelsky—JACK BENNY (comedian)
91. Irving Lahrheim—BERT LAHR (film star)
92. Pinkus Leff—PINKY LEE (TV star)
93. Gerold Lefkowitz—GEROLD FRANK (author of *The Boston Strangler*)
94. Steven Leibovitz—STEVE LAWRENCE (singer)
95. Israel Edwin Leopold—ED WYNN (film star)
96. Manfred Lepovsky—MANFRED LEE (creator of Ellery Queen)
97. Norman Levinson—NORMAN NORELL (fashion designer)
98. Joseph Levitch—JERRY LEWIS (comedian)
99. Marian Levy—PAULETTE GODDARD (film star)
100. Harold Lipshitz—HAL LINDEN (TV's Barney Miller)
101. Benjamin Liener—BENNY LEONARD (boxing champion)

102. Laszlo Lowenstein—PETER LORRE (film star)
103. David Los—DAVID LEWIS (leader of Canada's New Democratic Party)
104. Morton Saul Lyon—MORT SAHL (comedian)
105. Walter Matuskanschayak—WALTER MATTHAU (film star)
106. Jacob Maza—JACKIE MASON (comedian)
107. Bruce Meyerowitz—BRUCE MORROW (Cousin Brucie, formerly on New York's WABC radio)
108. Golda Meyerson—GOLDA MEIR (Israeli Prime Minister)
109. Morris Miller—ROBERT MERRILL (opera star)
110. Joan Molinsky—JOAN RIVERS (comedienne)
111. Alvin Morris—TONY MARTIN (entertainer)
112. Daniel Nathan—FREDERIC DANNAY (with Manfred Lee creator of Ellery Queen)
113. Peter Nierow—PETER NERO (pianist)
114. Ronald Nissenbaum—RON NESSEN (Pres. Gerald Ford's press secretary)
115. Yigal Paicovitch—YIGAL ALLON (Israeli politician)
116. Joseph Papirofsky—JOSEPH PAPP (Broadway producer and director)
117. Jacob Pincus Perelmuth—JAN PEERCE (opera star)
118. Betty Perske—LAUREN BACALL (film star)
119. Shimon Perske—SHIMON PERES (Israeli politician, Lauren Bacall's first cousin)
120. Michael Igor Peschlowsky—MIKE NICHOLS (film director)
121. Roberta Peterman—ROBERTA PETERS (opera star)
122. Borge Rosenbaum—VICTOR BORGE (comedian, pianist)
123. Lev Semiulovich Rosenberg—LEON BAKST (Russian artist)

124. Barnet David Rosovsky—BARNEY ROSS (boxing champion)
125. Dorothy Rothschild—DOROTHY PARKER (author and critic)
126. Jacob Rubenstein—JACK RUBY (killer of Lee Harvey Oswald)
127. Leonard Alfred Schneider—LENNY BRUCE (comedian)
128. Shirley Schrift—SHELLEY WINTERS (film star)
129. Bernard Schwartz—TONY CURTIS (film star)
130. Moshe Segal—MARC CHAGALL (artist)
131. Robby Segal—ROBBY BENSON (film star)
132. David Shapiro—DAVID FRYE (impressionist)
133. Mark Shapiro—MARK SHERA (J. R. Jones in TV's *Barnaby Jones* series)
134. Fanny Rose Shore—DINAH SHORE (TV star)
135. Milton Sills—SOUPY SALES (comedian)
136. Howard Silverblatt—HOWARD DA SILVA (actor)
137. Belle Silverman—BEVERLY SILLS (opera star)
138. Philip Silversmith—PHIL SILVERS (comedian)
139. David Slavitt—HENRY SUTTON (novelist)
140. Aubrey Solomon—ABBA EBAN (Israeli statesman)
141. Herbert Jay Solomon—HERBIE MANN (jazz musician)
142. Erich Oswald Stroheim—ERICH VON STROHEIM (film star, director)
143. Maier Suchowljansky—MEYER LANSKY (gangster)
144. William Szathmary—BILL DANA (comedian, famous for his character "José Jimenez")
145. Murray Teichman—ARTHUR MURRAY (dance instructor)
146. Irving Tennenbaum—IRVING STONE (novelist)
147. Judith Tuvim—JUDY HOLLIDAY (film star)

148. Bernard Valvrojenski—BERNARD BERENSON (art historian)
149. Meir Moiseevitch Wallach—MAXIM MAXIMOVITCH LITVINOV (Russian statesman)
150. David Wallace—DAVID WALLECHINSKY (editor of *The Book of Lists* and *The People's Almanac*. His father is novelist Irving Wallace; his grandfather was named Wallechinsky)
151. Nathan Weinstein—NATHANAEL WEST (novelist)
152. Eric Weiss—HARRY HOUDINI (escape artist)
153. Muni Weisenfreund—PAUL MUNI (film star)
154. Bernard Wessler—BERNIE WEST (producer of *The Jeffersons, Three's Company,* and other TV comedies)
155. Laibel Willcher—ARTHUR WELSH (pioneer aviator)
156. Lewis Winnowgradsky—SIR LEW GRADE (film director)
157. Yitzhak Yezernitsky—YITZHAK SHAMIR (Prime Minister of Israel)
158. Moe Zudecoff—BUDDY MORROW (swing bandleader)
159. Isaac Zylberman—ISAAC BASHEVIS SINGER (novelist)

Composer George Gershwin's father had his name changed from Gershowitz. Aaron Copland's father changed his from Kaplan. Bennett Cerf's paternal ancestors were named Hirsh. Hirsh means deer in Yiddish, as does Cerf in French. The father of Dr. Melvin Calvin, 1961 Nobel Prize-winner in chemistry, was originally named Kalvarisky.

FIFTY-TWO JEWISH ODDITIES

Some people you wouldn't have expected to be Jewish, or to have existed at all:

1. CHRISTOPHER COLUMBUS—There is considerable evidence that Columbus was a Marrano, a Jew who adopted Christianity to avoid death at the hands of the Spanish Inquisition (which, by the way, was instituted just months before Columbus's voyage) while secretly remaining true to his faith. Documents discovered in the Spanish town of Potevedra indicate that he was the son of Susanna Fonterosa, a Jewess. Columbus's selection of a number of known Jews among his crew and leaving a legacy in his will to "the Hebrew who lived at the gate of the Jewry" are among the many facts which support this theory.

2. THE PILGRIM—One of those who disembarked from the *Fortune,* a ship arriving at Plymouth from Amsterdam in 1621, was a Moses Simonson. One of his descendants, Rev. Paul Sturtevant Howe, claimed that Simonson was Jewish in a letter to the *Philadelphia Public Ledger* on November 15, 1920.

3. THE NAZI OFFICER—Oswald Rufeisen, a Polish Jew, managed to conceal his true identity during the Nazi occupation of Poland, enlisted in the German Army and became deputy to the military commander of the town of Mir, a position from which he aided his fellow Jews. During the course of the war, Rufeisen was exposed, escaped, and took refuge in a convent. He subsequently adopted Catholicism and became a Carmelite monk. As "Brother Daniel," his unsuccessful attempt to obtain Israeli citizenship under the Law of Return (which grants citizenship immediately to any Jew who requests it upon coming to Israel) became a *cause celèbre* in the 1950s.

4. THE INDIANS—A few thousand Indians scattered throughout Mexico are descendants of Marranos and native Mexican Indians whom they converted and intermarried with.

The group was not allowed to openly avow their religion until 1910, and as a result, the Judaism they practiced for centuries became distorted, picking up many Catholic and pagan rites along the way. In modern times they have shed most of these non-Jewish customs and maintained some contact with the mainstream of Mexican Jewry. Several hundred underwent formal conversion to Judaism in the 1950s and '60s.

5. THE POPE—Many legends abound concerning various medieval Popes who are claimed to have been Jews abducted as children and raised as Catholics. The stories are probably based on the fact that Pope Innocent II (1130–43) was indeed the descendant of Jews who adopted Christianity.

6. THE GRANDSON OF THE MAYOR OF GAZA—Rashad A–Shawa, grandson of Gaza's mayor of the same name, is, by Jewish law, a Jew. His mother, Susan, daughter of Rumanian Jewish parents, met his father, Zohar A–Shawa, while he was on a visit to London. She died in 1978 and was buried in Gaza's Moslem cemetery.

7. THE MATADOR—Brooklyn-born Sidney Franklin (né Frumkin) became the first non-Latin to succeed as a bullfighter. His career in Mexico and Spain spanned nearly forty years, during which time he became a close friend of bullfighting-enthusiast Ernest Hemingway.

   A Jew who followed in Franklin's footsteps was Randy Sasson who fought bulls in Colombia.

8. THE ATHEIST RABBI—Sherman T. Wine of the Birmingham Temple in Farmington, Michigan, created something of a sensation in the mid-1960s when the media picked up on his avowed atheism. His beliefs are set forth in his *Humanistic Judaism*.

A 1972 poll conducted by the Central Conference of American Rabbis showed that 14 percent of all American Reform rabbis admitted to being atheists or agnostics.

9. THE MAN WHO BROUGHT NASSER TO POWER—Joseph Rosenthal, the KGB's top agent in Cairo, was responsible for convincing the Kremlin to back Nasser in his rise to power in 1952. Toward the end of his life, Rosenthal espoused Zionism and emigrated to Israel.

10. THE QUEBEC SEPARATIST POLITICIAN—English-speaking David Levine is one of the Parti Québécois' few anglophones and Jews. In his 1979 election bid, he was swamped by his Liberal opponent by a margin of 23,254 to 791.

11. PABLO PICASSO—Picasso's Jewishness is not documented but it could be a fact. The late Israeli artist Moshe Bernstein maintained it was so. Bernstein, in his youth, was a member of the Paris clique of Jewish artists which included Chagall, Soutine, and Modigliani. "Picasso was one of us," he used to insist. "For years we breathed the same air. I know." Even then, maintained Bernstein, Picasso tried to hide his Jewishness. When asked if he was a Jew, Picasso once answered, "If Jews are persecuted, I am a Jew."

12. THE OIL TYCOON WHO WAS AMERICA'S LEADING TALMUDIC SCHOLAR—Soon after Bernard Revel arrived in America in 1906, Jews considered him the nation's leading young "talmid chochom" (Talmudic scholar). He married Sarah Travis, daughter of a pious Jew with vast oil holdings in Oklahoma. Sarah's father used to arrange for a minyan (ten adult Jewish men) to be with him at the oil fields so that he wouldn't have to miss communal prayers. Revel managed the Travis family's enterprises for a number of years before returning to New York to become the first president of Yeshiva University.

13. THE WILD WEST'S MOST POPULAR DANCE HALL QUEEN—
When Adah Mencken and her show came to town, the
miners and cowboys always turned out in droves. The
highlight of the evening came when Adah would make her
appearance strapped to the back of a horse, seemingly
dressed only in a pair of tights. She was the first performer
to wear a flesh-colored costume to give the illusion of nud-
ity. Mark Twain was among her most enthusiastic fans.

14. THE EMPEROR OF THE UNITED STATES—After losing the
fortune he amassed in the California Gold Rush, Joshua
Norton seems to have lost a few marbles as well. A familiar
sight walking around San Francisco in his uniform, "Emperor Norton," as he declared himself, spent the rest of his
life issuing decrees and levying taxes. Taxes under fifty
cents were generally paid, as the people of San Francisco
had a soft spot in their hearts for their Emperor.

     Upon his death in 1880, San Francisco rabbis forbade
Norton's burial in a Jewish cemetery because he proclaimed himself "King of the Jews." Twenty thousand San
Franciscans were present at his burial in a nondenomina-
tional cemetery. Norton's remains were recently moved to
a Jewish cemetery.

15. ADOLF HITLER'S DOCTOR—Dr. Eduard Bloch treated Hitler's family during his childhood. During his years as an
artist in Vienna, Hitler once sent Dr. Bloch two of his
paintings with an inscription expressing his eternal
gratitude.

16. THE TV STAR WHO ALWAYS WORE A YARMULKE—Former
yeshivah student Steven Hill (born Shlomo Berg) was the
first star of TV's popular *Mission Impossible* series. An
Orthodox Jew, he had to leave the show because it con-

flicted with his strict Sabbath observance. Hill always wore a yarmulke. When being filmed he concealed it under a toupee.

17. THE SOLE SURVIVOR OF THE BATTLE OF THE ALAMO—Louis Moses Rose was the only one of the Texas troops defending the Alamo who chose to escape rather than fight to the death. A French immigrant and veteran of the Napoleonic wars, he felt that he had already had more than his share of suffering in battle. While none of the primary sources for this story identify Rose as a Jew, his name indicates that he was. Other Jews who fought and died at the Alamo include a Dr. Levy, surgeon for the Texas troops, and an A. Wolf, in whose memory a monument stands in Austin, Texas.

18. PRESIDENT ASSAD'S HOUSEGUESTS—On a trip to Syria in 1977, Mexican Chief Rabbi Abraham Hershberg and his wife Rivkah spent the night at the house of President Assad after the Syrian ruler told them they wouldn't be safe at a hotel. The Hershbergs were in Syria to arrange for fifteen unmarried Syrian Jewish women to emigrate to the United States. With single women outnumbering single men in the Damascus community, they never would have been able to marry. The Hershbergs' mission was successful.

19. THE YOUNGEST AMERICAN SOLDIER IN WORLD WAR I— Benjamin Edelstein of Detroit served at the age of fifteen after lying about his age.

20. THE SHORTEST AMERICAN SOLDIER IN WORLD WAR II— Nissum Attas, a New Yorker from the Lower East Side, was four feet five inches tall.

21. JEWISH SOLDIERS WHO FOUGHT ON THE NAZI'S SIDE— When Germany attacked Russia, Finland fought alongside her to regain territory lost in the Russo–Finnish War. Fin-

land would not consent to German demands to remove Jews from its army, resulting in situations where Jewish soldiers actually reported to Nazi officers.

22. THE CATERER FOR PHILADELPHIA'S CELEBRATION OF THE RATIFICATION OF THE CONSTITUTION—It was the event of the year in 1788, and Isaac Moses was there in charge of the kosher table for Jewish participants. Among those who marched at the head of the parade that day was Rabbi Gershon Mendes Seixas of New York's Congregation Shearith Israel.

23. MISS AMERICA 1945—New York's Bess Myerson is the only Jewish Miss America. As of yet, no Jew has won the Miss Black America award. (Bert Parks, long-time MC of the Miss America Pageant, is also a Jew).

24. MISS UNIVERSE 1976—Israel's Rina Messinger. (While on the subject of beauty queens, up and coming film star Fran Drescher (*Saturday Night Fever, Ragtime*) was runner-up in the Miss New York Teenager contest in 1973.)

25. FIDEL CASTRO'S MINISTER OF COMMERCE—Castro appointed Maximo Bergman to the post in 1961, sacked him in 1962.

26. CHARLIE THE TUNA—Hershel Bernardi provides his voice.

27. THE JOLLY GREEN GIANT—Hershel Bernardi again.

28. MATCHMAKERS—The marriage of King Ferdinand of Aragon and Queen Isabella of Castille, perpetrators of one of history's most far-reaching and large scale acts of anti-Semitism, the expulsion of Jews from Spain, was arranged by two Jewish bankers, Abraham Senior of Castille and Solomon of Aragon.

29. PEACEMAKERS—In the early stages of World War I, England and Germany arranged a meeting between two of their most prominent Jews, Sir Ernest Cassel and Albert Ballin,

hoping that as "bloodbrothers" they would be able to arrive at some sort of *modus vivendi*.

30. WARMONGERS—When the Colombian government refused permission to dig the Panama Canal, Panama then being a part of Colombia, New York's Seligman banking house, which stood to make a large profit from the venture, financed a U.S. government inspired revolution in Panama, which led to Panamanian independence, and a cooperative government.

31. THE FIRST EUROPEAN TO SET FOOT IN THE NEW WORLD—Luis de Torres, Columbus' interpreter.

32. THE FATHER OF MODERN BOWLING—Louis B. Stein (1858–1949) instituted the 300 score and sixteen pound ball as standard in modern bowling.

33. THE MAN WHO BURIED HIS TEFILLIN AT THE SOUTH POLE—Roy Millenson of Bethseda, Md., buried his worn out *tefillin* (the proper means of disposal) in a hole in the snow of the South Pole on January 3, 1974. Millenson, then an aide to Sen. Jacob Javits, went to the South Pole on a congressional inspection of scientific installations.

34. THE FIRST JEW TO CHOOSE CREMATION INSTEAD OF BURIAL—Dr. Samuel Hahn of New York in 1908.

35. THE MAN WHO SOLD THE WORLD'S MOST VALUABLE STAMP—Irwin Weisberg sold an 1856 British Guiana one-cent stamp to an anonymous buyer in New York in 1980 for $850,000. He and eight partners bought the stamp in 1970 for $280,000.

36. THE WORLD'S BOUNCING CHAMPION—Sixteen-year-old Doron Menashe of Israel bounced a soccer ball on his foot 22,200 times in three hours without letting it drop in August 1980.

37. THE WORLD'S GREATEST CORONER—Dr. Milton Helpern,

chief medical examiner for the city of New York for 43 years, dissected over 20,000 human bodies and participated in over 50,000 autopsies. His opinion as to cause of death was considered the last word on the issue in thousands of criminal cases and insurance claims. Helpern died in 1977 at the age of 75.

38. MEYER LANSKY'S BODYGUARD—Israeli Yoske Shiner had previously served in that capacity for David Ben-Gurion.

39. THE CITIZEN OF THE WORLD—That's what Garry Davis, a well-known figure in the late 1940s and early '50s, was called. Soon after leaving the army at the conclusion of World War II, Davis founded the Association for the International Registry of World Citizens and People's Assembly, which advocated the dissolution of individual countries and the founding of a global government. He gained publicity through stunts such as burning his American passport and taking refuge in a United Nations office when French police were trying to apprehend him for being in the country without proper documents. Customs officials at Israel's Ben-Gurion Airport would not recognize Davis's passport, issued by the "World Service Authority," when he tried to enter the country in 1976.

40. THE PRESIDENTIAL CANDIDATE—Barry Commoner, son of Isidore Commoner and the former Goldie Yarmolinsky, finished fourth in the 1980 presidential elections on the Citizens Party ticket.

41. AMERICA'S MOST FAMOUS MONK—Brother Dominic, the character made famous by a series of Xerox commercials, is played by Brooklyn-born Jewish comedian Jack Eagle.

42. THE WEST POINT BAR MITZVAH BOY—Lyle Jay Kellman's parents were in the midst of divorce proceedings when he was thirteen, so his bar mitzvah was postponed until his

twenty-first birthday in 1981. He became the only West Point cadet ever to have his bar mitzvah there.

43. BEST CAB DRIVER IN NEW YORK—Stanley Epstein received this award at the Madison Avenue Sportscar Driving and Chowder Society Crosstown Rally on March 24, 1980.

44. ISRAEL'S MOST UNLIKELY GUEST—Dr. Hjalmar Shacht, Hitler's Minister of Finance, spent two hours at Lod Airport in November 1951, en route to Germany from Indonesia.

45. THE SAUDI PRINCE'S DOCTOR—In 1957, King Saud of Saudi Arabia took his polio-stricken son to New York to be treated by Dr. Henry Kessler. Dr. Kessler was not allowed into Saudi Arabia because he was a Jew.

46. ARAB GOVERNMENT MINISTERS—In 1956, two Jews held ministerial posts in Arab governments. Mr. Albert Bessis was Tunisia's Minister of Towns, and Dr. Leon Benzaken was Morocco's Minister of Posts.

47. THE OWNER OF NEW YORK'S TOUGHEST BAR—Murray Goldman, whose Terminal Bar in the Port Authority Bus Terminal area was given that title by *New York* magazine.

48. THE WORLD'S SMALLEST BABY TO SURVIVE—Chaya Snyder, of the Bronx, weighed in at 15 ounces at birth in September 1979. She was three-months premature.

49. THE WIFE OF EGYPT'S FOREIGN MINISTER—Mrs. Kamal Hassan Ali is the former Lea Nadler of Safed, Israel. The two met many years ago in Paris.

50. THE PRESIDENT OF THE MOONIES—Yiddish-speaking, Brooklyn-born Mose Durst is a leader in the Unification Church.

51. THE THREE-PIECE-SUIT BUSINESSMAN—Jerry Rubin, ex-Yippie leader, has gone "establishment." After a stint at the John Muir & Company stock brokerage firm, he left to establish his own investment business.

52. THE FUTURE CHIEF OF THE SIOUX—Little Sun Bordeaux, a

direct descendant of Chief Crazy Horse, is the son of a Jewish mother, Armalona Santos, who is raising him as a Jew. Little Sun attends classes at the religious school of Temple Shalom in Spokane, Washington. The Sioux believe he is a reincarnation of Crazy Horse.

EIGHTEEN JEWISH SUICIDES

1. SIMON LUX—This Czech writer shot himself in the chest in the Hall of the League of Nations in 1936 as an act of protest against the free world's appeasement and indifference toward Hitler.
2. RICHARD WISHNETSKY—This disturbed young man shot and killed Morris Adler, Detroit's leading Conservative rabbi, in the middle of Sabbath services on Lincoln's Birthday, 1966, and took his own life immediately afterward.
3. SAMSON—The biblical strongman took his own life, along with those of thousands of Philistines, when he brought down their temple.
4. THE DEFENDERS OF THE GARRISON AT MASADA—They committed mass suicide in 73 C.E. in face of certain defeat and enslavement at the hands of the Romans.
5. HANS HERZL—Theodore Herzl's son took his life after his sister Pauline died in 1930. The younger Herzl had led a troubled life and converted to Christianity. Trudy Herzl, Theodore's lone surviving child after Hans's death, was killed in Auschwitz along with her husband, Richard Neumann. Their only son, Richard Jr., Theodore Herzl's only grandchild and an American citizen, committed suicide after hearing of his parents' death.
6. THE GIRLS OF THE WARSAW GHETTO—A letter found in

Poland in 1975 tells of the abduction by the Nazis of 93 students of the Beth Yakov Religious School in 1942. Upon discovery that they were expected to become prostitutes for the SS, the entire group committed suicide by poison. The letter was written by one Chaya Friedman before she took her life.

7. KING SAUL—The first King of Israel had himself impaled on his own sword rather than be subjected to disgrace and torture at the hand of the enemy Philistines.

8-9. MEIR FEINSTEIN and MOSHE BARAZANI—Zionist guerrillas sentenced to death by the British, they blew themselves up in their Jerusalem prison cell in 1947.

10. OTTO WEININGER—This brilliant Austrian philosopher's classic work, *Sex and Character,* contained an attack on Judaism often quoted by Nazi propagandists. Having adopted Christianity upon graduating from the university, Weininger shot himself above the heart at the age of 23.

11. SZMUEL ZYGIELBOIM—A member of the Polish government-in-exile in London, he killed himself a few days after the Warsaw Ghetto uprising in protest against the free world's passivity in the face of the extermination of Europe's Jews.

12. THE JEWISH COMMUNITY OF YORK—Like their predecessors at Masada, the Jews of twelfth-century York, in England, chose to die by their own hands rather than at the hands of a Christian mob. Having fled to Clifford Tower where York's Christians besieged them, the Jews set the tower on fire. Over 500 perished.

13. SIMONE WEIL—This French philosopher, finding refuge in England in the face of the German occupation of her country, starved herself to death so that she could share in the suffering of the victims of Nazi persecution.

14. AVRAHAM OFER—Israel's Minister of Housing under the

Rabin government, Ofer shot himself after coming under suspicion of misappropriating the funds of a housing company he headed before joining the government.

15. ROMAIN GARY—The French novelist and diplomat shot himself in the head in December 1980, at the age of 66, a year after the suicide of his ex-wife, actress Jean Seberg.

16. FRANZ SONDHEIMER—The noted chemist, winner of the Israel Prize in 1961, took cyanide in February 1981, after a prolonged depression.

17. ROGER ANNENBERG—The only son of Walter Annenberg, former U.S. ambassador to Great Britain, took his life in 1962, at the age of 24.

18. ADAM CZERNIAKOW—Head of the Warsaw *Judenrat,* the Jewish "self-governing" body under Nazi rule, he took poison on the eve of the first deportations from the Warsaw Ghetto, July 23, 1942. His diary, recently published in English, has been called the most important diary to emerge from the Holocaust.

Two American-Jewish Doctors Who Also Authored Best-Sellers and Were Murdered by Persons from Greater Washington in 1980

1. HERMAN TARNOWER—Author of *The Complete Scarsdale Medical Diet* was murdered by Jean Struve Harris, headmistress of the Madeira School, a place where Washington's elite send their daughters. Harris shot Tarnower, her paramour, after he dropped her for another woman.

2. MICHAEL HALBERSTAM—Author of *The Wanting of Levine,* a thriller about America's first Jewish President. Halberstam

was shot by Bernard Charles Welch, Jr., a master criminal, whose robberies in the Washington area netted him goods valued at several millions of dollars. Halberstam ran Welch down with his car, injuring him, before dying of his gunshot wounds.

FIVE DEFENDANTS REPRESENTED BY JEWISH LAWYERS

1. CHARLES MANSON—In the famous 1970 murder trial, Manson was defended by Irving Kanarek, a Los Angeles lawyer known for his obstructionist tactics. Prosecutor Vince Bugliosi acknowledged that Kanarek was the most capable of the defense lawyers involved in the case.
2. THE CHICAGO SEVEN—These young radicals were defended against charges of conspiracy to incite violence at the 1968 Democratic Convention by William Kunstler in a trial lasting from September 1969 through February 1970. Five of the seven were found guilty of incitement, none of conspiracy. Kunstler has acted as defense counsel for many other leftists, including the Black Panthers, and Philip and David Berrigan. His grandfather, Dr. Joseph Mandelbaum, was team physician for the New York Giants.
3. MARK DAVID CHAPMAN—John Lennon's assassin was defended by Herbert J. Adelberg, who asked to be removed from the case after being hounded by crank callers. He was replaced by Jonathan Marks.
4. GEORGE LINCOLN ROCKWELL—In a 1966 trial on charges of disorderly conduct, the fuehrer of the American Nazi Party was defended by Martin Berger, foreshadowing a 1978 case when a gang of Chicago Nazis was represented by lawyers

supplied by the largely Jewish American Civil Liberties Union.

5. SIRHAN SIRHAN—Robert Kennedy's assassin was defended by Emile Zola Berman.

TWENTY-THREE JEWISH HEADS OF STATE AND HEADS OF GOVERNMENT OUTSIDE ISRAEL

1. LEON BLUM—Prime Minister of France 1936–37.
2. ANDREW COHEN—Governor of Uganda, 1953–56.
3. BENJAMIN DISRAELI*—Prime Minister of Great Britain, 1868, 1874–80.
4. KURT EISNER—Prime Minister of the short-lived Bavarian Socialist Republic which seceded from Germany, 1918–19.
5. SIR JOSHUA ABRAHAM HASSAN—Current Prime Minister of Gibraltar.
6. ALICE HEINE—She shared the throne of Monaco with Prince Albert I, great-grandfather of today's Prince Rainier, from 1880 until 1902 when Prince Albert divorced her.
7. SIR ISAAC ISAACS—Governor-General of Australia, 1930–36.
8. BRUNO KREISKY—Chancellor of Austria, 1970–83.
9. BELA KUN—Head of Hungary's short-lived Communist government of 1919.
10. EUGENE LEVINE—Succeeded Kurt Eisner as Prime Minister of the Bavarian Socialist Republic in 1919.
11. LUIGI LUZZATTI—Prime Minister of Italy, 1910.
12. DAVID MARSHALL—Chief Minister of Singapore, 1955–56.
13. RENE MAYER—Prime Minister of France, 1953.
14. PIERRE MENDES-FRANCE—Prime Minister of France, 1954–55.

15. JULIUS POPPER—A Rumanian Jew who managed an Argentine mining company, Popper obtained the gold mining rights in Tierra del Fuego in 1887 and proceeded to declare it an independent kingdom with himself as king. The Argentine navy put his reign to an end shortly thereafter.

16. JOSE LOPEZ PORTILLO—In an article published in the Israeli newspaper *Yediot Achronot* in September 1977, Mexico's President claimed his mother was Jewish. If this is true, Portillo would be considered a Jew by Jewish law.

17. MATYAS RAKOSI—Communist dictator of Hungary, 1949-56.

18. LORD READING—Viceroy of India, 1921-26.

19. SIDNEY SONNINO—Prime Minister of Italy, 1906, 1909-10.

20. SIR JULIUS VOGEL—Prime Minister of New Zealand, 1873-76.

21. SIR ROY WELENSKY—Prime Minister of the Central African Federation (Rhodesia and Nyasaland), 1956.

22. ZELMAN COWEN—Governor-General of Australia, 1977-82.

23. MALCOLM FRASER—Prime Minister of Australia, 1976-83. While he doesn't consider himself Jewish, his maternal grandmother was a Jew, thus rendering him Jewish by the standards of Jewish law.

Former Portuguese Prime Minister Mario Soares is descended from Marranos, secret Jews who adopted Christianity under the Inquisition. S. D. Emanuel, Prime Minister of Surinam in the early '60s, claimed his ancestors were Jewish though he himself was not.

---

*See Converts to Christianity

THREE JEWS IN THE FRENCH CABINET

The current French government, headed by President François Mitterand and Prime Minister Pierre Mauroy, includes the following Jewish members:

1. PIERRE DREYFUS—Minister of Industry.
2. ROBERT BADINTER—Minister of Justice.
3. CHARLES FITTERMAN—Minister of State in charge of transportation (Fitterman is the second highest-ranking member of the French Communist Party.)

French Jewish film star Roger Hamin is married to Mitterand's sister Christine.

EIGHT PROMINENT NINETEENTH-CENTURY AUSTRALIAN JEWS

While Australia's nineteenth-century Jewish population never exceeded 15,000, the following Jews were born there or lived there for many years:

1. SIR SAMUEL ALEXANDER—The greatest of all Australian philosophers.
2. SIR JULIUS VOGEL—Premier of the province of South Australia, later Prime Minister of New Zealand.
3. SIR JOHN MONASH—Australia's greatest military leader.
4. V. L. SOLOMON—Premier of the province of South Australia.
5. JOSEPH JACOBS—Editor of the *Jewish Encyclopedia* and a founder of the Jewish Historical Society of England.
6. SIR ISAAC ISAACS—Governor-General of Australia.
7. BARNETT LEVY—Opened Australia's first theater.
8. JOHN HARRIS—Founder of Australia's police force in the late eighteenth century.

Six Jews Named David Horowitz

1. Ex-NBC news correspondent, currently a television consumer advocate in Los Angeles.
2. New York-based ABC television executive
3. Former NBC director of financial planning
4. Former editor of *Ramparts* magazine and co-author of the best-seller *The Rockefellers*
5. U.N. journalist, writer of the syndicated column "Behind the Scenes at the U.N."
6. Former director-general of Israel's Ministry of Finance

Source: *New West* magazine, Jan. 28, 1980.

Sixteen English Words Derived from Hebrew

1. AIR—From the Hebrew *avir* (air)
2. CAMEL—From *gamel* (camel)
3. CHECKMATE—A combination of words *shach* (sheikh or shah, e.g., king) and *met* (dead)
4. CIDER—From *shechar* (hard drink or beer)
5. COTTON—From *kutonet* (jacket)
6. GAUZE—From the French *gaze,* thought somehow to derive from Gaza
7. HAREM—From the Hebrew *cherem* (off limits)
8. JUBILEE—From the Hebrew *yovel* (jubilee)
9. METAL—From the Greek *metallon,* thought to derive from the Hebrew *matekhet* (metal)
10. PARADISE—From the Hebrew *pardes* (orchard)
11. SACK—Taken directly from Hebrew
12. SAPPHIRE—From the Hebrew *sapir*

13. SCALLION—From the Israeli town Ashkelon
14. SIDE—From the Hebrew *tsod*
15. TURKEY—Rabbi Lee J. Levinger in *A History of the Jews in the United States,* claims that Luis Torres, a Jewish member of Columbus's crew, coined the word, a corruption of the Hebrew *tuki* (parrot)
16. WINE—From the Latin *vino,* derived from the Hebrew *yayin* (wine)

JEWISH POPULATION OF EUROPEAN* CITIES (est.)
*(including USSR)

Amsterdam	20,000	Liverpool	6,500
Antwerp	13,000	London	280,000
Athens	2,800	Lvov	40,000
Basle	2,500	Lyons	20,000
Belgrade	1,500	Marseilles	65,000
Berlin	6,000	Manchester	35,000
Birmingham	6,000	Milan	10,000
Bordeaux	6,400	Minsk	47,000
Brussels	24,500	Moscow	285,000
Bucharest	40,000	Nice	20,000
Budapest	65,000	Odessa	120,000
Copenhagen	6,000	Paris	300,000
Czernowitz	70,000	Riga	40,000
Glasgow	13,000	Rome	15,000
Istanbul	22,000	Stockholm	8,000
Kharkov	80,000	Strasbourg	12,000
Kiev	170,000	Toulouse	18,000
Kovno (Kaunas)	8,000	Vienna	9,000
Leeds	18,000	Warsaw	5,000
Leningrad	165,000	Zurich	6,100

Jewish Population of the Continents (est.)

North America 6,360,000
South America 675,000
Europe (incl. USSR) 4,000,000
Asia 3,190,000
Africa 200,000
Oceania 80,000
World total 14,505,000

Two Jewish Child Prodigies

1. LEONARD ROSS—In 1956, this twelve-year-old astounded American television viewers with his mastery of the intricacies of the stock market, as he went on to win the top prize on *The $64,000 Question*. He was a guest at the Democratic National Convention that year. Ross is also the youngest person ever awarded a ham radio operator's license, earning his at the age of nine.

2. EUGENE VOLOKH—This twelve-year-old sophomore with an I.Q. of 206 is U.C.L.A.'s youngest undergraduate. He and his parents emigrated to the United States from Russia when he was seven. Eugene pulls all As in his science and math classes and works as a computer programmer in his spare time.

2.
Conversion to and from Judaism

FOURTEEN CONVERTS TO JUDAISM

1. DIANE FEINSTEIN—Mayor of San Francisco. Feinstein, whose father is Jewish and mother Roman Catholic converted to Judaism at the age of twenty.
2. GALIA BEN-GURION—A native Israeli and veteran of the Israeli army, David Ben-Gurion's granddaughter had to undergo conversion before her marriage, when the Israeli rabbinate discovered that her mother's conversion was invalid, thereby rendering her non-Jewish according to Israeli law.
3. EDUARD KUZNETSOV—One of the Prisoners of Zion involved in the famous Russian-American prisoner exchange of 1979, Kuznetsov had to undergo conversion to Judaism upon his arrival in Israel, though he had been active in Jewish causes for most of his adult life. Kuznetsov's father was Jewish, but his mother was not.

4. ELIZABETH TAYLOR—She was converted by Dr. Max Nussbaum of Los Angeles' Temple Israel before she wed Eddie Fisher. Her later marriage to Richard Burton was a Unitarian ceremony .

5. MARILYN MONROE—Dr. Robert Goldburg of New Haven, Connecticut, converted her before her marriage to playwright Arthur Miller.

6. WARDER CRESSON—Born a Quaker, Cresson developed an interest in Judaism through his association with Isaac Leeser, leader of Philadelphia's Orthodox Jewish community, which he followed up in 1844 by becoming the first American consul to Palestine. When his term as consul ended in 1848, Cresson converted to Judaism. Upon his return to the United States in 1849, his family had him declared legally insane, a decision which was appealed and subsequently overturned. Cresson returned to Jerusalem, married a Jewish woman, and became a prominent figure in the Sephardic community.

7. REUEL ABRAHAM—Born Karl Schneider, this Luftwaffe pilot converted to Judaism after completing a self-imposed twenty-year penance for his role in World War II.

8. AULCIE PERRY—Formerly of the Virginia Squires team, Aulcie, or Elisha ben Avraham as he is now known, is one of Israel's top basketball stars. A few years ago, rival teams tried to discredit him by spreading rumors that his conversion was invalid.

9. SAMMY DAVIS, JR.—Converted by Dr. Max Nussbaum (the man who brought you Liz Taylor), Davis talks about the path that led him to Judaism in his autobiography *Yes, I Can.*

10. LORD GEORGE GORDON—One of history's most celebrated converts, Gordon was a member of the House of Lords

who adopted Judaism in 1787. While behavior of this sort was rather peculiar for a British nobleman of his time, there is no truth to the allegation that he was insane.

11. ABRAHAM SETSUZAU KOTSUJI—Born an adherent of Shinto, Kotsuji converted to Presbyterianism and became a master of the Hebrew language, tutoring Emperor Hirohito's brother in that subject. He became a Jew after World War II.

12. DOLORES ANN SHULMANN—The former Dolores Ann Baker, a cousin of Henry Cabot Lodge, she converted to marry an Israeli, Yuval Shulmann.

13. JOHN NEWMAN—The catcher for the Oakland Athletics may be the only major league ballplayer who has ever converted to Judaism.

14. ULRIKE KOHOUT—A victim of the August 29, 1981, PLO attack on Vienna's Stadttempel synagogue. Kohout was killed while trying to protect a friend's two-year-old son. She converted to Judaism two years before her death.

SIX JEWISH ORCHESTRA CONDUCTORS WHO CONVERTED TO CHRISTIANITY

Conducting was a field closed to Jews in pre-World War II Europe. As a result a number of talented Jewish musicians underwent baptism, usually as a mere formality to advance their careers. Among those who converted:

1. OTTO KLEMPERER
2. SERGE KOUSSEVITSKY
3. GUSTAV MAHLER
4. PIERRE MONTEUX
5. EUGENE ORMANDY
6. SIR GEORGE HENSCHEL

Things have changed a bit since those days, though. Not long ago, Israeli Eli Jaffe conducted at London's Albert Hall wearing a yarmulke (skullcap) and with his tzitzis (the fringed, four-cornered garment worn by Orthodox Jewish men) clearly visible.

NINE RABBIS WHO CONVERTED TO CHRISTIANITY

1. ANTON ZOLLI—The former Chief Rabbi of Rome, he became a Franciscan monk after World War II.
2. MAX WERTHEIMER—One of the first graduates of Cincinnati's Hebrew Union College, Wertheimer served as rabbi of Dayton's Reform congregation before becoming a Baptist minister in 1904.
3. RUDOLF HERMANN GURLAND—Born Chaim Kurland, he served as the rabbi of Wilkomir, Lithuania, before being baptized into the Russian Orthodox faith in the late nineteenth century. He officiated as an Orthodox priest in towns throughout Russia and was active in missionary work among Jews.
4. SAM STERN—Imprisoned in a concentration camp as a young man, after receiving his rabbinic ordination Stern served as a rabbi in a displaced-persons camp before moving on to accept a pulpit in Rhode Island where he became a "Hebrew-Christian." He is currently a missionary in Los Angeles.
5. DON PABLO DE SANTA MARIA—Born Solomon Levi, this fifteenth-century rabbi and Talmudic scholar adopted Catholicism and went on to become a vicious persecutor of Jews from his position as archbishop of Burgos, Spain, the town he had previously served as chief rabbi.
6. CHARLES FRESHMAN—As a young Hungarian immigrant in

the 1890s, Freshman served as rabbi of the Jewish community of the city of Quebec. The local community was scandalized when he was baptized in the Wesleyan Methodist Church, going on to become a minister of that sect.

7. JACOB FRESHMAN—One of America's earliest Jewish Christian missionaries, he operated on New York's Lower East Side in the 1880s, with little success.

8. HERMAN PAUL FOREST—A former rabbi of Poughkeepsie, New York, he headed the Hebrew-Christian Mission of the Allen Street Presbyterian Church, which was active on the Lower East Side in the 1890s.

9. JOHANNES ISAAC LEVITA—A sixteenth-century German rabbi who became a Catholic and taught Hebrew at the universities of Louvain and Cologne. Levita also worked for Christophe Plantin, a Catholic printer who created some of the most beautiful Hebrew typefaces ever made.

Sources: *Good News Magazine; Encyclopedia Judaica;* Irving Howe, *World of Our Fathers; The Jerusalem Post*

TWENTY-SEVEN OTHER JEWS WHO CONVERTED TO CHRISTIANITY

1. KARL MARX—Converted to Christianity by his father at the age of six, Marx later expressed contempt for the Jews as the epitome of bourgeois capitalism.

2. REV. WESLEY FRENSDORFF—First bishop of the Nevada Episcopal diocese, Frensdorff is the son of German Jews who were killed in the concentration camps.

3. JUDAH TOURO—The great early-American philanthropist was a convert to Episcopalianism. Ironically, one of the

handful of liberal arts colleges in the United States under Orthodox Jewish auspices is named after him.

4. BORIS PASTERNAK—The author of *Doctor Zhivago* adopted Christianity after his disillusionment with Judaism, due, in large part, to being witness to the wholesale persecution of Jews in Eastern Europe during the first half of the twentieth century.

5. JAMES SCHLESINGER—A cabinet member in both the Ford and Carter administrations, Schlesinger became a Lutheran while in college.

6. MARCEL DASSAULT—The baron of the French aircraft industry is a convert to Catholicism.

7. JEAN-MARIE LUSTIGER—Archbishop of Paris. Hidden from the Nazis as a child by a Catholic family, Lustiger adopted the religion of his foster parents. He was recently quoted as saying, "I was born a Jew and I shall remain one even if this fact is difficult to accept by some. I continue to consider myself Jewish even if the rabbis do not agree to this."

8. BOBBY FISCHER—The chess champion, born Jewish, is a member of the Worldwide Church of G—d, Protestant.

9. BENJAMIN DISRAELI—Baptized by his father at the age of thirteen, Disraeli retained a lifelong identification with what he referred to as "the Jewish race."

10. BOB DYLAN—He once accepted a well-known Jew as his savior in 1979 when he joined the Vineyard Christian Fellowship. He recently abandoned Christianity and renewed his interest in Orthodox Judaism.

11. MICHAEL SOLOMON ALEXANDER—Born Michael Solomon Pollack and raised as an Orthodox Jew, Alexander converted to Christianity and became Anglican bishop of Jerusalem in 1841. He engaged in missionary activity among Jews.

12. SARAH BERNHARDT—The leading French actress of the late nineteenth and early twentieth centuries, she was converted at the age of twelve but always remained proud of her Jewish heritage.

13. HEINRICH HEINE—Heine's conversion at the age of 28, motivated by the hope of advancing his career, was a source of embarrassment to him for the rest of his life.

Interestingly enough, in April 1966, a twenty-year-old German woman descended from Heine was converted to Judaism by an Israeli rabbinic court.

14. MICHAEL BLUMENTHAL—Jimmy Carter's first Secretary of the Treasury was converted to Presbyterianism as a child.

15. M. ROBERT GUGGENHEIM—One of the many members of New York's richest Jewish family who became Christians. Upon hearing of his conversion, his father is reported to have remarked, "I'm delighted. Robert was always a very bad Jew. I'm sure he'll make a fine Catholic."

16.–18. ABRAHAM MENDELSSOHN, HENRIETTE MENDELSSOHN, and DOROTHEA MENDELSSOHN-SCHLEGEL—Children of Moses Mendelssohn, father of Reform Judaism, they adopted Christianity as did Mendelssohn's grandsons, Johann and Philip Veit.

19. JOE ROSENTHAL—The photographer famous for his shot of the flag raising on Iwo Jima is a convert to Catholicism.

20. PHIL KING—The first Jew named to an All-American football team (while playing for Princeton in 1890) and the first Jew to coach college football (for Wisconsin in 1896).

21. JUDAH MONIS—The first Jewish graduate of Harvard (1720), he became a Protestant so that he could get a job there teaching Hebrew.

22. GIANCARLO UZZIELLI—Husband of the former Anne Ford.

23. EMIN PASHA—Born Edward Schnitzer, this Polish Jew, bap-

tized as a child, was colonial governor of Egypt in the nineteenth century.

24. ROBERT NEUMANN—The recent U.S. ambassador to Saudi Arabia converted to Catholicism in 1933, at the age of seventeen, in his native Vienna. Neumann spent a number of months in the Dachau and Buchenwald concentration camps but claims he was imprisoned for being a Socialist rather than a Jew. Neumann is generally considered to have been among the more pro-Arab officials in the State Department.

25. JACQUES (JACOB) OFFENBACH—The popular nineteenth-century composer had to become a Catholic before his fiancée's stepfather would allow them to marry.

26. ARLO GUTHRIE—The son of Woody Guthrie, is best known for his song "Alice's Restaurant."

27. LEWIS NAMIER—One of England's foremost historians, a staunch champion of Zionism and foe of anti-Semitism. His conversion to the Russian Orthodox Church in 1947, at the insistence of his fiancée, sent shock waves through Britain's Jewish community.

EIGHT POLEMICAL WORKS AGAINST CHRISTIANITY WRITTEN BY JEWS

The Jewish literary tradition of polemics against Christianity finds its source in medieval times when Christian monarchs forced Jews to attend church sermons, and rabbis to debate priests. The earliest of these polemics were records of these debates, but the tradition has continued down to modern times and will endure as long as there is Christian proselytizing among Jews. The following list is limited to works available in English.

1. NACHMANIDES' DISPUTATION—The record of a debate be-

tween Nachmanides and a Spanish priest initiated by King James I of Aragon. This is clearly the most famous work of its kind. It is one of the rare instances where Christians acknowledged the Jew to be the winner. An English translation can be found in *Writings and Discourses of Nachmanides,* translated by C. B. Chavel, Shilo Publishing House, 1978.

2. THE DISPUTATION—An adaption of *Nachmanides' Disputation* to contemporary times by an anonymous author. Published by Scholarly Publications, 1972.

3. THE JEWISH—CHRISTIAN DEBATE IN THE HIGH MIDDLE AGES: A CRITICAL EDITION OF NIZZAHON VETUS, WITH AN INTRODUCTION, TRANSLATION, AND COMMENTARY BY DAVID BERGER—The first English translation of this anonymous medieval work, is a classic in the genre. Published by The Jewish Publication Society, 1980.

4. FAITH STRENGTHENED—By Isaac Troki. This critique of Christian arguments against Judaism, written by a sixteenth-century Lithuanian Jew of the Karaite sect (which accepted Biblical law literally and rejected the rabbinic tradition), is the most comprehensive, and, according to most experts, best work of its kind. First translated into English in London in 1850, it was reissued in 1970 by the Hermon Press and is currently in print.

5. IS CHRISTIANITY THE FULFILLMENT OF JUDAISM?—By Dov Heller, Aish HaTorah Publications, 1979. The author of this booklet has unique credentials. Raised in a Reform home, he found no spiritual satisfaction in the Judaism he was exposed to. He became a Christian and was ordained a Presbyterian minister by the Harvard Divinity School. On a trip to Jerusalem, Heller found his way to a yeshivah, where, after five years of study, he was ordained an Orthodox rabbi.

6. JEWS AND "JEWISH CHRISTIANITY"—By David Berger and Michael Wychogrod, Ktav Publishing House, New York, 1978. Clear and concise reasons why Jews should not become Christians, this book is unique in its tone of respect and sensitivity toward the position of the Jew turning in that direction. If a book can get a "Jewish Christian" to change his mind, this is probably the one.

7. CONSCIENCE ON TRIAL—By Morris Braude, Exposition Press, New York, 1962. A collection of medieval disputations between rabbis and priests.

8. THE BOOK OF THE COVENANT—By Joseph Kimhi. Translated by Frank Talmage; Pontifical Institute of Medieval Studies, Toronto, 1972. An early Jewish polemic against Christianity.

EIGHTEEN NON-JEWS COMMONLY THOUGHT TO BE OR TO HAVE BEEN JEWISH

1. THOMAS MASARYK—Pre-World War II President of Czechoslovakia. The Nazis spread the rumor that he and his wife were Jewish.

2. WERNER HANS ERHARD—It seems to be common knowledge that the founder of est is Jewish. Well, not exactly. He was born John Paul Rosenberg and his father was Jewish, but his mother wasn't.

3. JULES VERNE—He was amused by the rumor that he was a Polish Jew and sometimes played along with it.

4. LEO GORCEY—The actor who played the role of Spit Mahoney, leader of the Bowery Boys and the Dead End Kids, is not Jewish, but his father, Bernard Gorcey, who played candy store owner Louie Dombrowski in the Bowery Boys

films, was. On the subject of the Bowery Boys, one who made good was Sidney Lumet (he's Jewish), currently a top Hollywood director. Among the Bowery Boys' more illustrious co-stars was Ronald Reagan who appeared with them in "Hell's Kitchen" in 1939.

5. MAX BRUCH—The German composer has been wrongly alleged to be a Jew because one of his works is entitled "Kol Nidre" and his name sounds like the Hebrew name Baruch.

6. SEN. BARRY GOLDWATER—Goldwater, whose grandfather Michael Goldwasser was indeed Jewish, has often been referred to as a Jew, especially during his 1964 bid for the presidency.

7. SEN. WILLIAM COHEN—His father is Jewish.

8. MAX BAER—The heavyweight champ wore trunks with the Star of David on them to give the impression that he was Jewish because it was good for business.

   Former world lightweight champ Mike Rossman, who also sports the Star of David, is really Mike De Piano and goes to a Catholic church. Rossman, however, is his mother's maiden name. She's Jewish and considers her boy as such. Another Jewish boxer who displayed the Star of David on his trunks was Robert Cohen, who fought in the 1950s.

9. DAVID BERKOWITZ—"Son of Sam," the ".45 Caliber Killer," is the adopted son of Sam Berkowitz but is not of Jewish ancestry.

10. COL. MUAMAR QADAFFI—A persistent rumor in Israel has it that Qadaffi's supposedly Jewish mother was kidnapped and raped by Moslems, giving birth to her little Muamar. There is no evidence that this is true.

11. MICHAEL LANDON—He was born Eugene Orowitz and his

father was a Jew, but the *Bonanza* star's mother wasn't.

12. WILHELM MARR—A rabid anti-Semite and coiner of the term anti-Semitism, Marr is commonly, though mistakenly, alleged to be of Jewish descent.

13. ALEXANDRE DUMAS—His mother's maiden name was Lebay, not Levy.

14. JOSEPH PULITZER—His father was Jewish. He wasn't.

15. DMITRI MENDELEYEV—The pioneer geneticist was the son of a Russian Orthodox priest. He is thought to be a Jew because of the "Mendel" in his name.

16. MAURICE RAVEL—His name sounds like "Rav," Hebrew for rabbi.

17. HARRY BELAFONTE—The popular singer is the grandson of a Jew and married to one but is not Jewish himself.

18. ROMAN POLANSKI—Film director, and husband of the late Sharon Tate. Polanski's father was a Russian Jew, his mother a Polish Catholic. He considers himself Polish rather than Jewish. Both of Polanski's parents perished in Auschwitz. His father saved Roman's life by arranging for him to live with Polish Christian friends throughout the duration of World War II.

Charlie Chaplin would have wanted me to put his name on this list, but I just can't. Despite denying it for most of his life, Chaplin was Jewish. A venerable Lithuanian rabbi, who served for many years on London's East End, used to tell of the conversation he once had with novelist Israel Zangwill. Zangwill, who once taught in a *heder* (religious school for young boys) on the East End, told him that one of his pupils was none other than the "Little Tramp." A discussion of Chaplin's Jewish origins can be found in *The Universal Jewish Encyclopedia*.

THREE BOOKS ON STOPPING INTERMARRIAGE

1. WHY BE JEWISH?: INTERMARRIAGE, ASSIMILATION, AND
   ALIENATION—By Meir Kahane. A penetrating analysis of the
   greatest problems confronting contemporary American
   Jewry.
2. HOW TO STOP AN INTERMARRIAGE—By Kalman Packouz.
   The most practical book on the subject by a pioneer in the
   field. Rabbi Packouz, director of St. Louis' Aish Hatorah
   Center for Jewish Studies, is currently engaged in combating
   intermarriage through his Jewish Computer Dating Service.
   He was recently featured on NBC-TV's *Today* show.
3. INTERMARRIAGE—By Rabbi Jacob J. Hecht. A booklet put
   out by the National Committee for Furtherance of Jewish
   Education of the Lubavitch Hasidim, containing basic arguments against intermarriage.

3.
Anti-Semitism and Philo-Semitism

TEN GENTILES WHO WORE JEWISH SYMBOLS

1. HENRY MILLER—The author of *Tropic of Cancer* and other works once banned in the United States used to wear a silver mezuzah given to him by a Jewish friend.
2. SLY STONE—This soul-music star performs with a Star of David medallion hanging from his neck.
3. ROD CAREW—When the photograph of the American League's leading hitter over the past decade appeared on the cover of *Time*, a Hebrew *chai* (life) pendant was clearly visible. Carew is married to the former Marilyn Levy of Minneapolis.
4. LIONEL HAMPTON—He has a Star of David emblazoned on his xylophone case.
5. COUNT BASIE—This jazz master wears a *chai* pendant as an expression of affection for the Jewish people.
6. KING CHRISTIAN X OF DENMARK—When occupying Nazi forces decreed that all Jews must wear yellow badges, the

king wore one himself. The public at large followed his lead, rendering the decree meaningless.

7. REDD FOXX—The star of "Sanford and Son" often wears a gold *mogen Dovid* around his neck.
8. MAX BAER—The heavyweight champ had a Star of David sewn on his boxing trunks.
9. DAVE KINGMAN—One of baseball's top sluggers wears a *chai* medallion and mezuzah necklace.
10. ELVIS PRESLEY—Toward the end of his life, "The King" used to wear a *chai* medallion along with his crucifix.

THREE GENTILES WHO HAD THEMSELVES CIRCUMCISED AS A SIGN OF IDENTIFICATION WITH JEWS

1. ELAGABALUS—This Roman Emperor felt that circumcision was the most appropriate means of showing respect for the Jewish religion.
2. DON LOPE DE RIVERA—This early sixteenth-century Spaniard became fanatically pro-Jewish as a reaction to the Inquisition. Before being burnt at the stake for his sympathies, he performed circumcision on himself in his prison cell.
3. KOZO OKAMOTO—The only survivor of the Japanese terrorist squad who killed 26 at Lod Airport in 1972, Okamoto attempted to circumcise himself with a nail clipper in his prison cell in September 1974, after reading extensively about Judaism. A prison doctor finished off Kozo's sloppy job.

Sources: (1) M. Hirsh Goldberg, *The Jewish Connection;* (2) Stephen Birmingham, *The Grandees;* (3) widely reported in the Israeli press.

TEN "RIGHTEOUS PEOPLE"

In their attempt to exterminate European Jewry, the Germans met with little opposition among most of the peoples of Europe and were even given considerable assistance, particularly by Eastern Europeans. Hundreds of Gentiles in occupied countries, however, risked their lives to save their Jewish neighbors. Yad Vashem, an institute in Jerusalem devoted to commemorating the Holocaust, has recognized their efforts by awarding "Righteous People" citations to the deserving. Among the recipients:

1. ANTONI JAKUBOWSKI—As punishment for aiding Jews, the Germans had this Polish Catholic declared a Jew, changed his name to Aaron Levi, and sent him to his death.
2. VICTOR KUGLER—He hid the family of Anne Frank in Amsterdam for 25 months.
3. ONA SIMAITE—This Lithuanian librarian worked to rescue Jews from the Vilna ghettos. She survived Dachau and settled in Israel among some of those she saved.
4. EBERHARD HELMRICHT—A major in the Wehrmacht, Helmricht set up a farm in Poland on which he used to shelter Jews fleeing from concentration camps.
5. ANDRZEV KOWALSKI—He concealed six Jewish families throughout the war but was forced to leave his home afterward to escape persecution at the hands of Polish anti-Semites.
6. RAOUL WALLENBERG—A member of the Swedish diplomatic mission to Hungary, Wallenberg made superhuman efforts to bring Jews under the protection of Swedish diplomatic immunity by cramming them into buildings rented by the Swedes and thus saved tens of thousands of

lives. Wallenberg was taken prisoner by the invading Russians at the end of the war and has not been heard from since.

7. ANNA BORKOWSKA—Mother Superior of a convent in Vilna, she defied the orders of her superiors in the Catholic hierarchy and hid Jews in the convent throughout the war. Embittered by her experiences, she left the convent when the war ended. Though action of this sort by a nun normally brings with it excommunication, the church made an exception in Anna Borkowska's case.

8-9. MARIA CHOLEVA and KLEOPATRA MINOS—These two sisters were active in the Greek underground. When three Jewish members of the Palestine Brigade, taken prisoner by the Germans, jumped the train taking them to a German concentration camp as the train passed through Greece, Minos and Choleva hid them for months and assisted them in their escape.

10. ARISTIDES DE SOUSA MENDES—Serving as Portugal's consul in Paris at the time of the Nazi occupation, Mendes defied orders from Lisbon and worked night and day issuing visas to desperate French Jews. For his efforts, he was sacked by the foreign service and died in penury.

FOUR QUOTES FROM THE CARTER BROTHERS

1. There's a hell of a lot more Arabs than there is Jews.—Billy
2. They (his Jewish critics) can kiss my ass.—Billy
3. The Jewish media tears up the Arab countries full time, as you well know.—Billy
4. I know that he (Billy) is not anti-Semitic and has never made a serious, critical remark against Jews or other people in our country.—Jimmy

NINE MODERN JEWISH ANTI-SEMITES

History records numerous instances of Jews who have turned against their own people. Pablo Christiani, a Jew who became a Dominican monk, had the Jew badge instituted in thirteenth-century France. The apostate Johannes Pfefferkorn was the most notorious Jew-baiter of sixteenth-century Germany. Jacob Brafman, an apostate in Czarist Russia, wrote *The Book of Kahal*, the world's most popular anti-Semitic tract until the publication of the *Protocols of the Elders of Zion*. In more recent times, we have seen the following:

1. DANIEL BURROS—Organizer for the Ku Klux Klan in New York and a former National Secretary of the American Nazi Party, Burros killed himself in 1965 after *The New York Times* revealed that he was a Jew. Burros attended afternoon classes and had his bar mitzvah at a Queens synagogue.
2. IAN LEHR—A member of the American Nazi Party, Lehr was arrested for illegal possession of weapons in New York in 1963. He spent the night of his brother's bar mitzvah party in jail.
3. ELIEZER GRUENBAUM—Son of Yitzhak Gruenbaum, Israel's first Minister of the Interior, Gruenbaum was Auschwitz's most notorious *kapo*. He is the model for the character of Fruchtenbaum in K. Tzetnik's novel of Auschwitz *Call Him Feifel*. Gruenbaum survived the Holocaust and was killed in Israel by a Jewish avenger in 1948. His father had him memorialized in the *Scrolls of Fire*, a volume issued in memory of those who fell in Israel's War of Independence.
4. KAMAL NIMARI—The son of a Jewish mother and an Arab father, Nimari is a terrorist of the Palestine Liberation Organ-

ization who was apprehended by Israeli forces after murdering a nightwatchman in a village outside Jerusalem in 1975. Nimari used to maintain contact with his Israeli Jewish relatives before he got caught. He was released in a prisoner exchange in 1978.

5. WILLIAM NASSER—The subject of an article in the May 1969, issue of *The Arab World*, Nasser is another P.L.O. terrorist, the son of a Jewish mother and a Palestinian Christian father. He was captured by Israeli forces in March 1968 and is currently serving a life sentence in an Israeli prison.

6. MAURICE LEON—A New York Jew of French descent, he believed that German Jews were at the head of a worldwide conspiracy for world domination. He made an obsession of collecting "evidence" to support his theory, which he provided to Henry Ford, who made use of it in numerous anti-Semitic publications.

7. JEAN-GABRIEL COHN-BENDIT—This French leftist, brother of Daniel Cohn-Bendit, leader of the 1968 Paris student riots, has recently taken to promoting the theories of Robert Faurisson, a French professor of literature who has written a book maintaining that the notion of gas chambers and the extermination of Jews in concentration camps is all a big hoax.

8. MORITZ SCHARF—Principal witness in Hungary's notorious Tiszaeszlar blood libel trial of 1883. A young girl was found murdered in the town of Tiszaeszlar. Scharf, a teenager, testified that he saw his father and some other Jews slaughter the girl to use her blood for ritual purposes. In fact, a Christian neighbor of Scharf's killed the girl after raping her. Scharf, who discovered the secret, was in love with the murderer's daughter. The killer promised him her hand in marriage if he would testify in his favor. Scharf hated his father and chose to accuse him of the crime. The Jews were

acquitted after a lengthy trial during which experts on both sides tried to prove or disprove the notion that Jews commit ritual murder. In his later years, Scharf expressed regret for his actions. He remained a practicing Jew all his life and died in Amsterdam in 1929.

9. AARON BRIMAN—An apostate Jew, he provided Father August Rohling, founder of Austria's Anti-Semite Party and one of the experts called to testify in the Tiszaeszlar trial, with much of his "evidence" that Jews use Christian blood in their Passover matzos.

One of the most virulent anti-Semites of the late nineteenth century was composer Richard Wagner. Wagner's stepfather, and according to some scholars his natural father, was a Jew, Ludwig Geyer.

A CHRONOLOGY OF AMERICAN ANTI-SEMITISM

1743—A New York mob attacks a Jewish funeral procession.

1746—Philadelphia's Jewish cemetery is vandalized.

1776—Early 1800s: Many of the original thirteen states limit the right to vote or hold office to Christians.

1815—Pres. James Monroe recalls the American consul in Tunis, Mordechai Noah, for alleged misappropriation of federal funds to ransom non-Americans from pirates. In his letter of dismissal Monroe writes, "At the time of your appointment as consul at Tunis, it was not known that the religion you profess would form any obstacle to the exercise of your consular function."

1832—Georgia state representative James J. Stark calls Dr. Phillip Minis "a damned Jew who ought to be pissed on." Minis kills Stark in a duel.

1844—Governor Hammond of North Carolina insists that residents of the state celebrate Thanksgiving by offering up
their devotions to Jesus Christ. A Jewish protest to the
governor's proclamation was met with a rude reply.

1850—A mob led by Irish policemen raids a New York apartment building occupied by Jews, beating many of the
tenants and stealing cash and jewelry.

1854—The United States ratifies a commercial treaty with the
Swiss Confederacy that bars Jews from residing or doing
business in parts of Switzerland, despite protests by
American Jews. The law was on the books until Switzerland rescinded its anti-Semitic legislation in 1874.

1857—Captain Uriah P. Levy is dismissed from the U.S. Navy.
A board of inquiry reinstates Levy after his dismissal is
determined to have been motivated by anti-Semitism.

1862—Gen. U. S. Grant issues "Order No. 11," expelling all
Jews from the Department of Tennessee.

1872—A. J. Stewart, New York's largest department store,
insists that Jewish employees work on the High Holy
Days, firing those who do not. This policy is changed in
1873.

1872—A Jew, B. F. Waterman, is barred from serving in the
New York State Militia.

1877—The Grand Union Hotel, of Saratoga, New York, refuses
to admit Joseph Seligman, a prominent Jewish banker.
The affair becomes a *cause celèbre*, dominating the
news for weeks. Jews organize a boycott of the A. J.
Stewart department store, managed by Judge Henry
Hilton, owner of the Grand Union. Hilton, in panic,
makes a $1,000 contribution to Jewish charities but to no
avail, as the boycott continues and the store eventually
has to be sold.

1892—Jewish immigrants sent to Fall River, Massachusetts, are quickly dispersed to other towns amid rumors of an imminent pogrom.

1904—Polish residents of Chicago declare an unsuccessful boycott against Jewish businesses.

1904–1905—Melvil Dewey, state librarian of New York and formulator of the Dewey decimal system for classifying books, distributes a brochure for a Lake Placid resort, of which he was president, advertising that it would not accept Jewish clientele. Louis Marshall, one of American Jewry's leading spokesmen, leads a protest resulting in Dewey's censure by the Board of Regents of the University of the State of New York.

1907—Police commissioner of New York causes an uproar by writing in the *North American Review* that Jews commit 50 percent of the crimes in New York while comprising only 25 percent of the population. Statistics show that in that year Jews had actually committed only 16 percent of the crimes in the city.

1913—The B'nai Brith establishes the Anti-Defamation League to combat anti-Semitism.

1915—The only lynching of a Jew in America. Leo Frank, manager of an Atlanta pencil factory, was accused of the rape-murder of a fourteen-year-old employee. Tom Watson, a populist demagogue later elected to the U.S. Senate, inflamed the local populace against Frank. The evidence pointed to the guilt of a Gentile worker at the factory, who, it turns out, had confessed to the crime to his attorney, but the jury found Frank guilty, due to threats against them should the verdict turn out otherwise. Frank's death sentence was commuted to life imprisonment by Gov. John Slaton, who was convinced of his innocence. Slaton was forced to flee Georgia three days later. Egged on by Watson, a mob dragged Frank from his prison cell and lynched him near his alleged victim's home.

1916—*The Passing of the Great Race,* by Madison Grant, a book propounding Nordic superiority, is a best seller.

1916–1920—All major American film companies agree not to produce films which portray Jews negatively.

1918—From a U.S. Army manual: "The foreign born, and especially Jews, are more apt to malinger than the native born."

1919—New York University adopts the quota system. When that school's junior class elects a number of Jews to class offices, the administration nullifies the election.

1920—Henry Ford takes off on an eight-year spree of anti-Semitism in which his newspaper, the *Dearborn Independent,* prints the fraudulent *Protocols of the Elders of Zion* and regularly publishes charges of Jewish conspiracy to dominate America. When faced with an ugly libel suit because of his attacks against Aaron Sapiro, a Chicago lawyer, Ford chooses to settle out of court, stops publishing the *Dearborn Independent,* and makes a public apology.

1921—Cap. Robert Rosenbluth is arrested for the murder of Maj. Alexander Cronkhite in 1918. Cronkhite had accidentally shot himself at a pistol range where he and Rosenbluth were practicing. After a three-year-long trial, the court determines that there was not a shred of evidence against Rosenbluth, and there were no grounds for his arrest. The case is referred to as an American Dreyfuss Affair.

1923—President Eliot of Harvard proposes a quota on the number of Jewish students admitted in order to preserve the American character of the school. In the face of opposition from the university's board of governors and a threat by the Massachusetts statehouse to stop considering donations to Harvard tax deductible, Eliot does not carry out his proposal.

1924—Congress passes the Immigration Act, designed to halt Jewish and Italian immigration.

1927—Three Jewish interns at Brooklyn's Kings County Hospital are dunked in tubs of cold water by Christian physicians. One of the perpetrators explains that the hospital is "an institution which will not tolerate Jews."

1928—When a four-year-old girl disappears in Massena, New York, on the day before Yom Kippur, the town's rabbi is questioned by local police about the "Jewish practice of human sacrifice," and vigilantes search Jewish stores for the girl. The girl, who had wandered off into the woods and became lost, is found unharmed the next day. The mayor, however, subsequently tries to institute a boycott of Jewish merchants.

1929—Cottages at a Jewish-frequented resort near Milwaukee are burned and looted after the owner receives anti-Semitic threats.

1930–1940—American anti-Semitism reaches its peak, partly as a reaction to the Depression. Professional bigots such as Gerald L. K. Smith, William Dudley Pelley, and the "radio priest" Father Charles Coughlin command followings of hundreds of thousands. The openly pro-Nazi German-American Bund meets with success among immigrants from Germany but to a much lesser degree with second-generation Americans of German descent. (Jewish thugs from Murder, Inc., often used to break up Bund rallies.)

1939—A poll shows that 83 percent of Americans are opposed to taking in Jewish refugees from Europe.

1941—Col. Charles Lindbergh, spokesman for the America

First Committee, claims that Jews are pushing America toward war with Germany.

1943—A poll shows that 25 percent of Americans feel that Jews are less patriotic than other Americans.

1946—Rabbi Stephen A. Wise attacks Columbia University for placing an unofficial quota on Jewish students. Faced with a possible loss of its tax exemption, Columbia removes the question of religion from its application forms.

1946-1950—Major Faubion Bowers, the officer in charge of the personal security of Gen. Douglas MacArthur while the latter was serving as Supreme Commander for the Allied Powers in Japan, claims that the general referred to Franklin Delano Roosevelt as "Rosenfeld" and called Truman "that Jew in the White House." William Manchester, MacArthur's biographer, says that other intimates of MacArthur claim that he was completely free of any form of racism or bigotry. Obviously carried away by admiration for his subject, Manchester asserts that even if Bowers's allegations are true, they reflect "benign anti-Semitism" on MacArthur's part.

1948—Polls show that 21 percent of Americans feel that Jews have too much political power.

1950—The State Department agrees not to send Jewish servicemen to Dharan Air Base in Saudi Arabia.

1957-1959—There is a rash of bombings and attempted bombings of synagogues in the South.

1960—Six hundred forty-three reported incidents of swastika daubings on synagogues and cemeteries take place in the months of January and February.

1964—Black leader Malcolm X: "In America the Jews sap the

very lifeblood of the so-called Negro to maintain the State of Israel, its armies, and its continued aggression against our brothers in the East."

1964—Curtis B. Dall, Franklin D. Roosevelt's son-in-law, sues columnist Jack Anderson for reporting that he delivered an anti-Semitic diatribe before the Senate Finance Committee. Dall testified that certain legislation was being promoted by "political Zionist planners for absolute rule via one-world government." He claimed that his statement was anti-Zionist rather than anti-Semitic. Federal District Judge Alexander Holtzoff dismissed the case.

1965—Stephen Smith, brother-in-law of Robert and Ted Kennedy, is criticized by members of R.F.K.'s staff for frequenting a resort that discriminates against Jews.

1965—At a Greenwich Village gathering, musician Archie Shepp and poet LeRoi Jones launch into a tirade demeaning the slayings of civil rights activists Michael Schwerner and Andrew Goodman and criticizing Jewish preoccupation with the Holocaust. Interestingly enough, Jones had previously been married to a Jewish woman and has two children by her.

1967—In a school board election in Wayne, N.J., Newton Miller, a member of the board, urges voters to vote against other board members because they are Jewish. Miller apologizes for hurting the Jews' feelings but does not retract his statement. The Jews are turned out of office.

1969—A survey shows that 8 percent of Americans would definitely not vote for a presidential candidate if he was Jewish, with 6 percent undecided.

1972—*Medical Arts and Letters,* the New York State Journal of Medicine, publishes an article claiming that medieval English Jews committed ritual murder.

1973—Sen. William Saxbe of Ohio, commenting on linking U.S. trade with the Communist bloc to Russia's allowing Jews to emigrate, says, "If the Zionist Jews think that we are going to fight to the last drop of the farmer's blood, then I'm not going to be part of it."

1973—"Those Jewboys are everywhere. You can't stop them."— Richard Nixon in a taped conversation with John Dean on March 23.

1974—Attorney General William Saxbe: "One of the changes that's come about is because of the Jewish intellectual, who was in those days [1940s and '50s] very enamored of the Communist Party."

1974—Anti-Semitic pamphlets are distributed in Irish Catholic neighborhoods in Chicago attacking William Singer, Mayor Richard Daley's rival in the Democratic primary.

1974—Chairman of the Joint Chiefs of Staff, Gen. George S. Brown, on Jewish influence in America: "It's so strong you wouldn't believe it. We have the Israelis coming to us for equipment. We say we can't possibly get Congress to support a program like that. They say, 'Don't worry about Congress. We'll take care of Congress.' Now this is somebody from another country, but they can do it. They own, you know, large banks in this country, the newspapers. You just look at where the Jewish money is in this country."

1975—The U.S. Army Corps of Engineers refuses to use Jews in a Saudi Arabian project.

1980—Neo-Nazis set a blaze that destroys the sanctuary of Temple Beth David in Temple City, California.

1981—Los Angeles' Simon Weisenthal Center for Holocaust Studies is daubed with swastikas and anti-Semitic slogans.

Sources: About two thirds of the entries in this list are based on *A Promise to Keep*, by Nathan C. Belth, and *The Land That I Show You*, by Stanley Feldstein.

TWO BOOKS BY JEWS ALLEGING ZIONIST COLLABORATION WITH THE NAZIS

1. PERFIDY—1961 book by noted playwright and screenwriter Ben Hecht.

   The main thesis of this well-documented book is that the Zionist establishment (Ben Gurion, Weizmann, et al.) did not do all it could have done to save Jews during the Holocaust in order to capitalize on the world's sympathy and because it did not want large-scale emigration of Orthodox, *shtetl* Jews to Palestine. Hecht himself was a supporter of the anti-establishment Revisionist Zionist movement led by Menachem Begin. A recently published edition of *Perfidy* includes articles rebutting some of Hecht's points.
2. THE HOLOCAUST VICTIMS ACCUSE—By Moshe Shonfeld. English edition published by Neturei Karta of America in 1977.

   Shrill in tone and crude in style (possibly the fault of the translator) *The Holocaust Victims Accuse* is nonetheless a frighteningly well-documented little book. Some of the material here is covered in *Perfidy,* whose theme it shares, but much of it is fresh.

SEVENTY TWO NATIONS WHICH CONDEMNED ZIONISM AS RACISM AT THE U.N. ON NOVEMBER 10, 1975

1. Afghanistan
2. Albania
3. Algeria
4. Bahrain
5. Bangladesh
6. Brazil
7. Bulgaria
8. Burundi
9. Byelorussia
10. Cambodia
11. Cameroon
12. Cape Verde
13. Chad
14. China
15. Congo
16. Cuba
17. Cyprus
18. Dahomey
19. Czechoslovakia
20. Egypt
21. Equatorial Guinea
22. Gambia
23. East Germany
24. Grenada
25. Guinea
26. Guinea-Bissau
27. Guyana
28. Hungary
29. India
30. Indonesia
31. Iran
32. Iraq
33. Jordan
34. Kuwait
35. Laos
36. Lebanon
37. Libya
38. Madagascar
39. Malaysia
40. Maldives
41. Mali
42. Malta
43. Mauritania
44. Mexico
45. Mongolia
46. Morocco
47. Mozambique
48. Niger
49. Nigeria
50. Oman
51. Pakistan
52. Poland
53. Portugal
54. Qatar
55. Ruanda
56. Sao Tomé-Principe
57. Saudi Arabia
58. Senegal

59. Somalia	66. Ukraine
60. Sri Lanka	67. U.S.S.R.
61. Sudan	68. United Arab Emirates
62. Syria	69. Tanzania
63. Tunisia	70. North Yemen
64. Turkey	71. South Yemen
65. Uganda	72. Yugoslavia

Just for the record, here's how the rest of the member nations voted:

ABSTAINING (24)—Botswana, Colombia, Ethiopia, Fiji, Ghana, Honduras, Jamaica, Japan, Kenya, Lesotho, Malawi, Nepal, Papua-New Guinea, Peru, Philippines, Rumania, Sierra Leone, Singapore, Swaziland, Togo, Upper Volta, Venezuela, Zaire, Zambia.

ABSENT (13)—Argentina, Bhutan, Bolivia, Burundi, Central African Republic, El Salvador, Greece, Guatemala, Panama, Paraguay, South Africa, Thailand, Trinidad-Tobago.

OPPOSED (29)—Australia, Austria, Bahamas, Barbados, Belgium, Britain, Canada, Costa Rica, Denmark, Dominican Republic, Ecuador, Finland, France, Haiti, Iceland, Ireland, Israel, Italy, Ivory Coast, Liberia, Luxembourg, The Netherlands, New Zealand, Nicaragua, Norway, Sweden, United States, Uruguay, West Germany.

TWO JEWS WHO PREDICTED THE HOLOCAUST

1. The Preacher of Kelm, a leading nineteenth-century Polish rabbi, once said in a sermon during the Franco-Prussian War:

The German won't merely persecute the Jews as a pas-
time or simply be an oppressor of the Jews. No, gentlemen.
He will make out of Jew-hatred a kind of [law], heaven forbid.
Take this to heart. Because on account of the sin of . . .
Geiger [one of the leaders of Reform Judaism in Germany]
there will arise a new [law], German-style, against the Jewish
people. And there, heaven forbid, it will be written, "Kill the
Jews! Kill even the best of them!" May G-d guard us and save
us.

> —recorded in *Memoirs* of Rabbi Jacob Maza, first
> published in book form in 1936, from a series of
> newspaper articles written years earlier.

2. Rabbi Meir Simcha of Dvinsk wrote in his biblical commentary *Meshech Chochma,* published in 1925: "Because he
   [the "enlightened" Jew] has replaced Jerusalem with Berlin,
   there will come a tempest that will wrench him from his
   trunk."

ELEVEN REACTIONS BY LEADERS OF THE FREE WORLD TO THE PLIGHT OF JEWS DURING THE HOLOCAUST

1. "We cannot turn our country into a sponge for Europe."—
   The Swiss minister of justice explaining his country's policy
   of returning refugees to their countries of origin.
2. "It seems to me wrong to support bringing children to this
   country at present."—Sir Alexander Cadogan's opinion
   about a plan to bring some European Jewish children to
   England.
3. "In my opinion, a disproportionate amount of the time of
   this office is wasted in dealing with these wailing Jews."—
   A.R. Dew, head of the Southern Department of the British
   Foreign Office.

4. "I took an oath to protect that flag [pointing to the Stars and Stripes] and obey the laws of my country, and you are asking me to break those laws."—U.S. Secretary of State Cordell Hull to Nahum Goldmann when the latter begged him to grant asylum to a ship of Jewish refugees which docked for refueling in Norfolk, Virginia, in 1940. The ship and all of its passengers had to return to Europe.

5. "I cannot recommend that we open the question of relaxing the provisions of our immigration laws and run the risk of a prolonged and bitter controversy in Congress on the immigration question, considering the generous quantity of refugees we have already received."—Secretary of State Hull in a communication to President Roosevelt.

6. "I cannot recommend that we bring in refugees as temporary visitors and thus lay ourselves open to possible charges of nullification or evasion of the national-origins principle embodied in the quota laws."—Secretary of State Hull in a communication to President Roosevelt.

7. "Regardless of in what country the Olympic Games are held, there will be some group, some religion, or some race, that can register a protest because of the action of the government of that country, past or present."—Avery Brundage of the U.S. Olympic Committee, commenting on a suggestion that the United States boycott the 1936 Berlin Olympics.

8. "A hundred thousand Jews! What am I to do with them? Where am I to put them?"—Lord Moyne, British minister in the Middle East, upon being informed of Adolf Eichmann's offer to trade 100,000 Jews for trucks, coffee, and soap. Moyne was assassinated by Palestinian Jews.

9. "It is not desirable or practical to recommend any change in the quota provisions of our immigration laws."—Samuel I. Rosenman, a Jewish advisor to President Roosevelt, on a

suggestion that immigration laws be eased to facilitate the entry of victims of Nazi persecution to the United States.

10. "I am convinced that there are those among them (Jewish refugees) who will engage in activities in the United States inimical to our institutions and that, willingly or unwillingly, some of them will serve the interests of foreign powers after their arrival in the United States. I feel strongly that under these circumstances our present policy of admitting so-called refugees on a very large scale is unsound and that before this war comes to an end we may have occasion to regret this so-called humanitarianism, which is likely to result in extensive sabotage and the loss of American lives and property and the crippling of our national defense program to the extent that such sabotage may be effective."— Lawrence Steinhardt, a Jew, U.S. Ambassador to the Soviet Union, in a letter to U.S. Undersecretary of State Breckenridge Long. On other occasions, Steinhardt referred to Eastern European Jews as a dangerous criminal element.

11. "If we do that (place money in escrow in Swiss banks for Nazi leaders until the end of the war in exchange for the lives of 60,000 Balkan Jews), the Jews of the world will be wanting us to make a similar offer in Poland and Germany. Hitler might well take us up on such an offer, and there simply are not enough ships in the world to handle them."— British Foreign Minister Anthony Eden.

Sources: Herbert Druks, *The Failure to Rescue;* Arthur Morse, *While Six Million Died;* Bernard Wasserstein, *Britain and the Jews of Europe 1939–1945.*

SEVEN MEN REVERED BY CATHOLICS AS SAINTS

1. ST. AGOBARD—The ninth-century Bishop of Lyons. Holy Roman Emperor Louis the Pious's tolerance toward the Jews disturbed him so, that he wrote the Emperor numerous letters about their odiousness and insolence, a theme often repeated in his sermons. "The Jews," writes Agobard, "are cursed and covered by malediction as by a cloak. The malediction has penetrated them as water in their entrails and oil in their bones. They are cursed in the city and cursed in the country, cursed in their coming and going. Cursed is the fruit of their loins, of their land, of their flocks. Cursed are their cellars, their granaries, their shops, their food, and the crumbs of their tables."

2. ST. AMBROSE—The residents of fifth-century Milan were so inspired by one of his sermons that they burned down the local synagogue, an act which he subsequently referred to with pride.

3. LITTLE ST. HUGH OF LINCOLN—Alleged to have been murdered by Jews in the thirteenth century so that his blood could be used for the baking of Passover matzos, Hugh was never formally beatified but was the object of devotion for centuries.

4. ST. JEROME—This fourth-century resident of Israel was on familiar terms with many rabbis and even studied Hebrew under their tutelage. Nonetheless, he refers to Jews as "serpents" and their prayers as "the braying of donkeys."

5. ST. SIMON STYLITES—G. F. Abbott remarked that this fifth-century ascetic, famous for having lived 36 years on top of a 50-foot pillar, renounced "all worldly luxuries except Jew hatred."

6. ST. JOHN CHRYSOSTOM ("THE GOLDEN MOUTHED")—Con-

sidered to be among the greatest of the church Fathers, John Chrysostom's homilies contain some of history's most vicious verbal attacks on Jews. A typical example: "Degeneracy and drunkenness have given them the character of the lusty goat and the pig. They know only one thing, to fill their bellies, get drunk, to kill and beat one another up . . . "

7. ST. VINCENT FERRER—A high-ranking official in the fifteenth-century Spanish Castilian government, Ferrer enacted a number of anti-Semitic laws, including the yellow Jew badge, which served as a prelude to the Inquisition.

Sources: Fr. Edward Flannery, *The Anguish of the Jews;* X. Malcolm Hay, *The Foot of Pride;* Stephen Birmingham, *The Grandees.*

FIVE PASSAGES FROM THE KORAN ABOUT JEWS

1. They (the Jews) say, "Our hearts are the wrappings which preserve G-d's words. We need no more." No, G-d's curse is upon them, for their heresy. Little is it that they believe. (II, 88)
2. Is it not true that every time they (the Jews) make a covenant, some party among them throws it aside? Most of them are faithless. (II, 100)
3. They (the Jews) will do you no harm aside from a small annoyance. If they come out to fight you they will show you their backs (II, 111)
4. When you proclaim your call to prayer, they (the Jews) take it as mockery and sport. That is because they are a people without understanding. (V, 61)
5. Fight those who do not believe in G-d or the Last Day, nor hold that forbidden which has been forbidden by G-d and his

prophet, nor acknowledge the religion of truth, even if they are People of the Book, until they pay tribute and feel themselves subdued. (IX, 29)

THREE QUOTES FROM MUHAMMAD ALI ON ISRAEL AND THE JEWS

1. "In my name and the name of all Muslims in America, I declare support for the Palestinian struggle to liberate their homeland and oust the Zionist invaders."—On a visit to a Palestinian refugee camp in southern Lebanon in March 1974.
2. "I am prepared to fight on your side and under your flag."—On a visit to Cairo in June 1964.
3. "They (the Jews and Zionists) control America. They control the world."—In a 1980 newspaper interview.

NINE ANTI-SEMITES (AND ONE PRO-SEMITE) WHO RECANTED

1. WILHELM MARR—Founder of the League of Anti-Semites in the 1870's and coiner of the term "anti-Semite," Marr later declared that his racist writings disgusted him.
2. ELDRIDGE CLEAVER—After spouting anti-Jewish and anti-Zionist propaganda during his years as a Black Panther leader, Cleaver changed his views after an extended stay in Algeria. He denounced the U.N.'s 1975 resolution equating Zionism with racism as "a travesty upon truth" and referred to Zionism as the "Jewish survival doctrine." He also said that Jews "have done more than any other people in history to expose and condemn racism."

3. COUNT HEINRICH VON COUDENHOVE-KALERGI—An anti-Semite in his youth, this turn-of-the-century Austrian diplomat became a leading foe of anti-Semitism. Coudenhove, a Catholic, used to leave mass on Good Friday when the prayer for "the perfidious Jews" was recited.

4. AMON CARTER—This Fort Worth millionaire used to refer to Dallas as "Jewtown" in editorials he wrote for his newspaper. In the years before he died, he never missed a local affair of the National Conference of Christians and Jews.

5. FRIEDRICH NIETZSCHE—The German philosopher expressed anti-Jewish feelings during the years of his friendship with composer Richard Wagner, a rabid anti-Semite. Later on he remarked that "to meet a Jew is a blessing, especially if one has lived among Germans."

6. FATHER CHARLES EDWARD COUGHLIN (maybe)—The notorious Roman Catholic priest, known for his Jew-baiting radio broadcasts in the 1930s, is reputed to have bought a $500 Israel Bond in 1977.

7. COLONEL NOROHIRO YASUE—The man who translated *The Protocols of the Elders of Zion* into Japanese. Prolonged study of international Jewry on behalf of the Japanese government led him to change his anti-Semitic views. In 1942, he helped thwart Nazi plans to exterminate the Jewish refugee community in Shanghai.

8. JOHN JAY CHAPMAN—This prominent nineteenth-century New England dramatist and poet was an avowed admirer of Jews, often heaping praise on them for their morality, industriousness, and ingenuity. All that ended when for the first time in his life he actually saw Jews at a New Jersey beach and discovered that they looked and behaved like anyone else. From that time on he denounced them as an inferior race.

9. HANS LUDWIG HELD—German historian and an outspoken anti-Semite. His research into the Jewish legend of the *golem* (a living man created from mud by kabbalists) brought him into contact with Chaim Bloch, a Viennese rabbi and scholar. The two became friends, and Held's views about the Jews changed drastically. His book on the *golem*, when it was published, was full of praise for the Jews. Held died in the Sachsenhausen concentration camp.

THREE DEROGATORY EPITHETS FOR THE JEWS ORIGINATED BY JEWS

1. SHEENY—Probably first used by Sephardic American Jews for German Jewish immigrants, whose names often ended with the syllable "schein."
2. KIKE—Probably first used by German-American Jews for Eastern European Jewish immigrants, whose names often ended with the syllable "ki."
3. VUZVUZ—A term used by Sephardic Israelis for Ashkenazim. From the Yiddish word "vus" (what).

SIX COMMON PREJUDICES AGAINST JEWS

1. Jews are all Communists.
2. Jews have all the money.
3. Jews have burdened Western man with a system of morals that generates guilt and neurosis.
4. Jews are too liberal and permissive.
5. Jews always stick to their own kind.
6. Jews are always trying to push their way in where they're not wanted.

4.
Sports

Ten Short Jewish Baseball Stories

1. John J. McGraw, manager of the New York Giants in the 1920s, desperately sought to find a Jewish baseball star to attract New York's large Jewish population away from his local rivals, the Brooklyn Dodgers and the New York Yankees. He signed more Jewish players than any other baseball executive of his time but met only disappointment with the likes of Mose Solomon, Phil Weintraub, Jack Levy, and Andy Cohen.
2. The first baseball game in Jerusalem was played by American residents on July 4, 1927, in honor of the 151st anniversary of American Independence and the fiftieth birthday of Judah K. Magnes, chancellor of Hebrew University, who played second base for the winning side.
3. In 1927, Barney Dreyfuss, Jewish owner of the National League champions, the Pittsburgh Pirates, fined his star outfielder, Hazen "Kiki" Cuyler, fifty dollars for not sliding into second base. Cuyler responded by making anti-Semitic remarks to Dreyfuss and his son Sam on a number of

occasions. Despite his value to the team, Dreyfuss had Cuyler benched throughout the 1927 World Series against the Yankees, who won in four straight games.

4. In 1934, with the Detroit Tigers battling for their first American League championship in 25 years, star first-baseman Hank Greenberg mentioned that he would prefer not to play on Rosh Hashanah, the Jewish New Year. The subsequent uproar among Tiger fans induced Hank to change his mind, and on Rosh Hashanah he went on to hit two home runs. With the pennant already clinched, nobody minded that Hank sat out the game played on Yom Kippur, the Day of Atonement.

5. In prison after being sentenced to death for passing nuclear secrets to the Russians, Ethel Rosenberg wrote to her husband Julius, "The victory of the Dodgers over the Phillies quickly restored my customary good spirits."

6. Dodger ace Sandy Koufax refused to pitch the first game of the 1965 World Series because it was scheduled for Yom Kippur. After he beat the Yankees his first time out, New York third-baseman Clete Boyer complained, "Why couldn't today have been a Jewish holiday?"

7. The Philadelphia Phillies once intentionally rescheduled a rained-out game with the Dodgers on Rosh Hashanah so that Koufax wouldn't pitch against them. The Phillies lost anyhow, and their slugger, Frank Thomas, suffered an injury that disabled him for the rest of the season. Koufax jokingly interpreted this as divine vengeance.

8. The 1970 New York Mets, at the initiative of manager Gil Hodges, donated $500 to a vandalized Brooklyn synagogue.

9. Ron Blomberg was determined not to miss services on the

first night of Rosh Hashanah in 1971. His team, the Yankees, was playing a home game against Cleveland that
afternoon and, with the score tied in the bottom of the
ninth, it looked like the game would go on past sundown.
With a runner on third, Blomberg singled home the winning
run and made it to shul on time. Blomberg was also the MC
of a syndicated radio show and would not allow the show to
be broadcast on Yom Kippur.

10. Infielder and catcher Moe Berg played major league ball in
    1923 and from 1926 to 1939. A graduate of Princeton,
    Columbia Law School, and the Sorbonne, he wrote a thesis
    on Sanskrit and spoke ten languages. A member of the
    Brooklyn Dodgers, Chicago White Sox, Cleveland Indians,
    Washington Senators, and Boston Red Sox, he rendered
    valuable service to the United States Government as an
    espionage agent during a tour of Japan before World War
    II. His exploits have been immortalized in the book *Moe
    Berg: Athlete, Scholar, Spy* by Louis Kaufman et al.

THREE MAJOR LEAGUE BASEBALL TEAMS THAT HAD THREE JEWS ON THE ROSTER AT THE SAME TIME

1. In 1955, Sandy Koufax, Larry Sherry, and Norm Sherry,
   were all members of the Brooklyn Dodgers.
2. In 1972, the Oakland Athletics featured pitcher Ken Holtz-
   man, first-baseman Mike Epstein, and outfielder Art
   Shamsky.
3. The 1978 Chicago White Sox had Ross Baumgarten, Steve
   Stone, and Ron Blomberg on their roster.

THREE JEWS WHO WON BASEBALL'S
MOST VALUABLE PLAYER AWARD

1. HANK GREENBERG—American League, 1935 and 1940.
2. AL ROSEN—American League, 1953.
3. SANDY KOUFAX—National League, 1963.
     Sports Magazine's Most Valuable Player in the World
   Series Award was won by Koufax of the Dodgers in 1963 and
   1965. Larry Sherry, also of the Dodgers, won the award in
   1959.

FOUR JEWISH MAJOR LEAGUE UMPIRES

1. DOLLY STARK—N.L.
2. STAN LANDIS—N.L.
3. AL FOREMAN—N.L.
4. ALAN CLARK—A.L.—The only Jewish umpire currently
   active.

ELEVEN JEWS INVOLVED IN ICE HOCKEY
AND ONE HOCKEY EXECUTIVE INVOLVED WITH JEWS

1. LARRY ZEIDEL—A defenseman who played with the Detroit
   Red Wings, Chicago Blackhawks, and Philadelphia Flyers
   in the 50s and 60s, Larry was brought up in an Orthodox
   home and was always proud of his Jewish heritage. He once
   went after one of the Boston Bruins, swinging his stick,
   when his opponent told him, "You're next for the ovens,
   Zeidel."
2. YURI LYAPKIN—Defenseman on Russia's 1976 Olympic
   Gold Medal team.

3. CECIL HART—Manager and coach of the Montreal Canadiens during their Stanley Cup wins in 1930 and 1931.

4. SAMMY ROTHSCHILD—The first Jew to play in the National Hockey League, with the 1925 Montreal Maroons.

5. BERNIE WOLF—Washington Capitols goalie, retired in 1980.

6. MIKE VEISOR—Hartford Whalers goalie, the only Jew currently playing in the National Hockey League.

7. LAWRIE NISKER—Rookie of the Year in the Eastern Hockey League, 1980.

8. MIKE GOBUTY—Owner of the Winnipeg Jets.

9. EDGAR and PETER BRONFMAN—Owners of the Montreal Canadiens.

10. IRVING GRUNDMAN—Managing Director of the Montreal Canadiens.

11. HY BULLER—Defenseman for the New York Rangers (1951–54), and the only Jew ever to be named to a N.H.L. All-Star team. Despite his talents on the ice, Buller's career was cut short because he couldn't adapt to the rough and brawling style of play common in the N.H.L. It has been suggested that a turning point in his career was the time he backed down from a fight with Ted Lindsay of the Detroit Red Wings. Which brings us to. . . .

12. TED LINDSAY—In 1978, Alan Ishakis was a 24-year-old accountant, an ardent Detroit Red Wing fan, and a strictly Sabbath-observant Jew. His joy at the Red Wings getting into the Stanley Cup playoffs was offset by his disappointment upon discovering that tickets to the playoff games were to go on sale on a Saturday, a day on which Jews are forbidden to make any purchases. Ishakis called the Red Wing office and described his plight to a secretary. A short while later, he received a call from none other than general manager Ted Lindsay, who told him he could pick up his tickets on Sunday at the Red Wing office. The day after

the game, Lindsay called Ishakis again to find out if he had a good time.

The story doesn't end here, though. Ishakis's co-workers at Detroit's Frederick Meat Packing Co. bought him a ticket to the $100-a-plate Ted Lindsay Testimonial Dinner. Ishakis couldn't eat the food, which wasn't kosher, but he did attend so that he could thank Ted Lindsay personally.

RING MAGAZINE'S TOP TEN JEWISH BOXERS OF ALL TIME (as listed in the December 1977 issue)

1. Bennie Leonard
2. Lew Tendler
3. Abe Attell
4. Sid Terris
5. Barney Ross
6. Jackie Fields
7. Maxie Rosenblum
8. Charley Phil Rosenberg
9. Solly Simon
10. Ruby Goldstein

FOUR TWENTIETH-CENTURY SAMSONS

1. JOSEPH GREENSTEIN—Because of his diminutive size (5'4"), Greenstein was billed as "The Mighty Atom." Most of his professional career was spent in the United States, though he was a Yiddish-speaking native of Poland. His most famous feat of strength was holding a plane back from taking off from the ground, a stunt he accomplished twice. He continued public performances of his strongman stunts on behalf of Zionist causes when he was well past 80. "The Mighty Atom" died in 1978.

2. SIGMUND BREITBART—A native of Baranovitz, Poland,

Breitbart's reputation as a modern-day Hercules brought him top-billing at New York's Palace Theater, the vaudeville capital of the world, in 1923. Among his feats was supporting several horses on a platform on his back while the band played "Kol Nidre." Breitbart died at the age of 42, having contracted blood poisoning after he cut his hand on a nail.

3. BERL LEVINE—A popular circus performer in Spanish-speaking countries, Levine called himself "The Second Breitbart." He, too, was a native of Poland.

4. ISAAC (IKE) BERGER—A native of Jerusalem, Berger won a gold medal in weightlifting for the American team in the 1956 Olympics, and took silver medals in 1960 and 1964.

SAM MENACKER'S LIST OF JEWISH PROFESSIONAL WRESTLERS

"Slammin' Sammy" Menacker (*menaker* in Hebrew means someone skilled in the art of removing nonkosher sinews from slaughtered animals) is one of the greatest experts in wrestling lore alive today., Let's let him present these biographical sketches pretty much in his own words:

"In my many years in the wrestling profession I've come across very few Jewish wrestlers, but they were excellent and did very well. Here's my list:"

AL KARASICK—A Russian Jew who was one of the best light heavyweight wrestlers in the world; he was a European champion. When Karasick went to Australia he became the Australian light heavyweight champ. He quit wrestling to become a successful promoter in Honolulu. He died in the early 1950s.

ABE COLMAN—Abe was born in Russia, migrated to Canada, and wrestled in the U.S.A. He was most famous in the 1930s. Abe was short, stocky, and very fast. His weight was about 225 when he was in his prime. At present he resides in New York City and is a referee. I guess his age is about 65.

ELI FISHER—Eli, born and reared in New York City, was a top football player and an excellent wrestler. He could have been world's champion, but his career was cut short by a kidney ailment which caused his death in about 1938.

BUTCH LEVY—Butch is from Minneapolis and was a top-notch wrestler, weighing in at about 250. He was a protegé of the greatest of them all, Strangler Lewis (not Jewish). Butch quit during the 1950s to go into business with his dad in Minneapolis.

RUFFY SILVERSTEIN—The greatest Jewish wrestler of all time. Ruffy weighed at the most about 210 lbs. but could defeat anyone at any weight. A native of Chicago, he was a captain in the U.S. Army Cavalry during World War II. He died in 1980, a victim of multiple sclerosis.

HERBIE FREEMAN—Herbie was a New Yorker, born in Brooklyn and raised there. He wrestled the best of them in New York at Madison Square Garden during the 1930s. He was most erudite and a graduate of City College of New York. Herbie later became a promoter in Washington, D.C. He died of a heart attack about 1963.

SAMMY STEIN—A native of Brooklyn, he was a top football player—one of the few football players who never attended college. He was a sensational drawing card in New York and made many motion pictures in Hollywood. He retired in California, went into the wholesale liquor business, and died in Las Vegas, Nevada, in the early '60s. Sammy Stein was the biggest wrestling attraction in the history of Australian wrestling, where he reigned supreme during the 1930s and early '40s.

RICKY STARR—This gentleman, a graduate of Purdue University, where he was a star wrestler, made a fortune in the wrestling game. He was, believe it or not, an excellent ballet dancer and about the fastest man on the wrestling mat. He was England's biggest star when he was there. He is now retired, and resides somewhere in the U.S. He was most active in the 1950s and '60s.

SLAMMIN' SAMMY MENACKER—Born and reared in Manhattan, Sam's first venture into professional sports was as a baseball player. However, he found wrestling more to his liking. Sam was at the top of his career in 1941. That's when he entered the U.S. Army as a private; he emerged a major in 1946. He went into promoting and TV sportscasting and is now considered one of the best wrestling telecasters in the business. Sam is also a veteran of seventeen motion pictures.

MARK LEWIN—Mark Lewin is now one of the top heavyweight wrestlers in the nation. He was also a top star in Australia, when he was there under the aegis of Sam Menacker. Coincidentally, Mark started his wrestling career in El Paso, Texas, when Menacker promoted wrestling in that city. Mark is virtually the only active Jewish wrestler today.

FORTY-SEVEN MEMBERS OF THE JEWISH SPORTS HALL OF FAME

The Jewish Sports Hall of Fame was founded in December 1978 and is located at the Wingate Institute for Physical Education, just north of Netanya, Israel, with a branch in Los Angeles. Members are:

Harold Abrahams, Great Britain, track-and-field
Mel Allen, USA, sportscaster
Arnold (Red) Auerbach, USA, basketball
Viktor Barna, Hungary, table tennis
Isaac Berger, USA, weightlifting
Angela Buxton, Great Britain, tennis
Lillian Copeland, USA, track-and-field
Barney Dreyfuss, USA, baseball
Jackie Fields, USA, boxing
Alfred Flatow, Germany, gymnastics
Benny Friedman, USA, football
Marshall Goldberg
Alexsandr Gomelsky, USSR, basketball
Eddie Gottlieb, USA, basketball
Hank Greenberg, USA, baseball
Alfred Hajos-Guttmann, Hungary, swimming
Bela Guttmann, Hungary, soccer
Ludwig Guttmann, Great Britain, sports medicine
Nat Holman, USA, basketball
Hirsch Jacobs, USA, horse racing
Jimmy Jacobs, USA, handball
Irving Jaffee, USA, ice skating (speed)
Elias Katz, Finland, track-and-field
Agnes Keleti, Hungary, gymnastics
Sandy Koufax, USA, baseball
Benny Leonard, USA, boxing
Harry Litwack, USA, basketball
Sid Luckman, USA, football
Hugo Meisl, Austria, soccer
Daniel Mendoza, Great Britain, boxing
Ron Mix, USA, football
Lawrence (Lon) Myers, USA, track-and-field
Zvi Nishri, Israel, physical education leader

Angelica Roseanu, Rumania, table tennis
Al Rosen, USA, baseball
Fanny Rosenfeld, Canada, track-and-field
Barney Ross, USA, boxing
Leon Rottman, Rumania, canoeing
Louis Rubenstein, Canada, ice skating (figure)
Abe Saperstein, USA, basketball
Dick Savitt, USA, tennis
Adolph (Dolph) Schayes, USA, basketball
Mark Spitz, USA, swimming
Eva Szekely, Hungary, swimming
Irina Kirszenstein-Szewinska, Poland, track-and-field
Sylvia Wene, USA, bowling
Henry Wittenberg, USA, wrestling

TWO JEWS WHO WON THE ASSOCIATED PRESS ATHLETE OF THE YEAR AWARD

1. SANDY KOUFAX—1963, 1965
2. MARK SPITZ—1972

5.
Soviet Jewry

TWENTY-SIX PROMINENT SOVIET JEWS

With the exception of some Middle Eastern countries, the Soviet Union is probably the most anti-Semitic nation on earth today. Nonetheless, a number of contemporary Russian Jews have risen to prominence in Soviet society. Among them:

1. MAYA PLISETSKAYA—prima ballerina of the Bolshoi Ballet
2. ALEKSANDR CHAKOVSKY—editor of *Literary Gazette* and Communist Party ideologue
3. EMIL GILELS—pianist
4. ARKADY PAIKIN—Russia's most popular comedian
5. VIKTOR SHKLOVSKY—literary scholar
6. VALENTIN ZORIN—Moscow TV commentator
7. VINIAMIN LEVICH— scientist
8. GEORGI ARBATOV—head of the Institute of the U.S.A. and Canada
9. ROMAN KARMEN—movie director
10. ROY MEDVEDEV—historian, dissident leader
11. EVGENII VINOKUROV—poet

12. ISAAK POMERANCHUK—physicist
13. BORIS SLUTSKY—poet
14. IZRAIL GELFAND—mathematician
15. YURI LYAPKIN—hockey star
16. BORIS VOLYNOV—cosmonaut
    (The only American Jewish astronauts are Dr. Judith Resnick and Dr. Jeffrey Hoffman, who have yet to make a space flight.)
17. LAZAR KAGANOVICH—former deputy prime minister (still alive, in his 80s)
18. LEONID KOGAN—violinist
19. YURI ARONOVICH—orchestral conductor
20. BORIS SPASSKY—chess champion
21. VICTOR BELY—composer and musicologist
22. ALEKSANDR GOMELSKY—coach of the 1964 and the 1968 Olympic basketball teams
23. SAVELI KRAMAROV—film star
    (Once one of the Soviet Union's top motion picture comedians, Kramarov has been out of a job since 1976 when he applied for permission to emigrate to Israel.)
24. ISAAC KAZARNOVSKI—chemist
25. VLADIMIR VEKSLER—physicist
26. VITALII GINZBURG—physicist

FIVE SOVIET JEWISH WOMEN

1. MRS. ANDREI SAKHAROV—Andrei Sakharov is married to Yelena Georgevna Bonner, a Jewish dissident activist. Sakharov's son-in-law, Efrem Yankelevitch, is also Jewish.
2. MARSHAL ZHUKOV'S DAUGHTER—The daughter of the commander-in-chief of Soviet forces in World War II married a

Soviet general who was the brother of Zionist poet Ahad Haam. They emigrated to Israel, where she and her children converted to Judaism.

3. MRS. YAKOV STALIN—Josef Stalin's daughter-in-law, Yulia, was a Jew. Stalin frowned upon the marriage and, after his son Yakov had been taken prisoner in battle, had Yulia imprisoned for "betraying him to the Germans." Stalin's daughter Svetlana Alliluyeva's first husband, Grigory Maximov, was also Jewish. Stalin never met him. He once told Svetlana, "That first husband of yours was thrown your way by the Zionists."

4. MRS. VYACHESLAV MOLOTOV—Foreign Minister of Russia at the outbreak of World War II, Vyacheslav Molotov rose to his position because Hitler would not sign a pact of cooperation with the Soviets while Molotov's predecessor, Maxim Litvinov, a Jew, was in office. Stalin jailed Molotov's Jewish wife in 1948 for allegedly being a Zionist spy.

5. DORA KAPLAN—A Moscow college student, she shot the Soviet dictator in 1924 for "destroying democracy in Russia." Lenin survived for a few months but eventually died of his wounds. Kaplan was executed by the Communists.

Sources—(1) Hedrick Smith, *The Russians; Chicago Jewish Post and Opinion,* February 22, 1980; (2) *Jewish Digest* (3) Svetlana Alliluyeva, *Twenty Letters to a Friend;* (4) Ibid; (5) *The Jewish Observer.*

A BASIC CHRONOLOGY OF SOVIET JEWRY

1917—The Tsar was overthrown in March. The Pale of Settlement, the area where Jews were forced to live, was abolished. More than 500 anti-Jewish laws passed during the 300-year reign of the Romanovs were abrogated. In November the Bolsheviks came to power, promising equality of all nationalities and the elimination of anti-Semitism.

1919—The government established the Yevsektsiya (Jewish Section) to oversee the liquidation of Jewish religious and national organizations.

1920—Within the Soviet Union's new borders were 2.5 million Jews.

1921—By the end of the Civil War 200,000 Jews had been killed, many in pogroms in the Ukraine.

1923-1924—3,000 Zionists in 150 Soviet cities were arrested and imprisoned.

1924—Programs were launched to settle Jews in agricultural settlements in the Crimea and southern Russia as a solution to the dislocation of tens of thousands who had lost jobs as traders and petty merchants after the Revolution.

1928—Jewish settlement began in Birobidzhan, a bleak region near the Manchurian border. In 1934 the area became officially known as the Jewish Autonomous District, though Jews were a small minority of the population, with no opportunity for religious or cultural self-development. Birobidzhan never attracted many Jews; in 1970 they numbered 12,000, less than 10 percent of the area's population.

Zionism and Jewish culture were attacked. Publication of books and materials in Hebrew was ended. A number of Zionists and Jewish writers were imprisoned or exiled to remote regions.

1932—160,000 Jewish children were studying the Soviet curriculum in Yiddish-language schools, primarily in the Ukraine and Byelorussia. By the end of the decade, however, all such schools were closed.

An internal passport, to be carried by all adult citizens, was introduced by Stalin. "Jew" was designated as a nationality, to be shown on the passport.

1936-1938—During the Great Terror many Jews, including a number who had been active in the Revolution, were among the victims of Stalin's purges.

1938—Publication of *Der Emes*, a leading Yiddish newspaper in Moscow, was ended. In 1941, publication of *Shtern* and *Oktyabr*, other major Yiddish newspapers, was also stopped.

1940—With the annexation of Czech, Polish and Rumanian territories and the Baltic states, the Jewish population in the U.S.S.R. exceeded 5 million.

1941-1945—1.5 million Jews were victims of the Nazis; 200,000 Soviet Jewish soldiers died in battle; 20,000 Jews fought as partisans; 145 Jews were awarded the nation's top military decoration—belying recent Soviet propaganda that Jews did not fight in the war but were "hiding in Tashkent."

1942—The Jewish Anti-Fascist Committee was formed, giving Soviet Jews their first organizational framework since the Jewish Section was disbanded in 1930. The committee's primary purpose, however, was to enlist financial support for the Soviet war effort from world Jewry and to present a bright picture of the situation of Soviet Jewry.

1947—In a speech at the United Nations, Andrei Gromyko announced Soviet support for a Jewish state in Palestine. "During the last war," Gromyko said, "the Jewish people underwent exceptional sorrow and suffering. . . .

It may well be asked if the U.N., in view of the difficult situation of hundreds of thousands of the surviving Jewish population, can fail to show an interest in the situation of these people, torn away from their homes and countries."

1948–1953—The "Black Years of Soviet Jewry." Solomon Mikhoels, chairman of the Anti-Fascist Committee, was killed by the secret police, though his death was reported as the result of an auto accident. Other leaders of the committee were accused of maintaining ties with "Zionism" and "American imperialism," and with planning the secession of the Crimea from the U.S.S.R. 431 Jewish intellectuals, including leading writers, poets, actors, and musicians, were imprisoned; few returned from the internment camps. In 1952, twenty-four outstanding writers and poets—Bergelson, Markish, Feffer, and others were tried secretly and executed. The period culminated in the so-called "Doctors' Plot," when prominent physicians, mostly Jewish, were arrested and charged with killing government leaders and plotting the murder of others, under the direction of foreign intelligence services and the "international bourgeois organization Joint" (American Jewish Joint Distribution Committee). A wave of anti-Semitism ensued and there were rumors that Stalin was planning the mass deportation of Jews to eastern Russia. Stalin's death in March 1953 brought the release of the doctors, a diminution in anti-Jewish sentiment and the release of hundreds of thousands of political prisoners, including 150,000 Jews. Thousands of Jews still continued to languish in camps.

1957—The Soviet authorities permitted 3,000 copies of a prayer book, *Siddur ha-Shalom,* to be printed—a rare exception to the practice of not permitting publication of any Jewish religious material.

1961—*Sovietish Heimland,* a Yiddish literary journal published monthly in Moscow, appeared. As an official publication, it printed only government-approved articles.

1961–1963—Of more than 160 persons sentenced to death for "economic crimes," 60 percent were Jewish, prompting protests by Bertrand Russell and other leading Western intellectuals.

1963—A viciously anti-Semitic book, *Judaism Without Embellishment,* by T.K. Kichko, was published by the Ukrainian Academy of Sciences. Dozens of other anti-Semitic books have since been published in the U.S.S.R. and distributed abroad.

1966—Premier Alexei Kosygin indicated that the U.S.S.R. would place no obstacles in the way of citizens who desired to reunite with relatives abroad. A rush for applications for exit visas, mostly from Jews, followed.

1967—The Six-Day War in the Middle East sparked a new sense of national pride among Soviet Jews. This was a turning point in the development of Jewish emigration and cultural identity movements. On the last day of the war, the U.S.S.R. severed diplomatic ties with Israel; they have not yet been restored.

1970—In a desperate effort to leave the country, a group of eleven Jews and two non-Jews sought to hijack a plane on an internal flight from Leningrad and divert it to the West. Authorities discovered the plan and arrested the group and its accomplices—thirty-four persons in Leningrad, Kishinev, and Riga. Two of them, Mark Dymshits and Edward Kuznetsov, were sentenced to death, but their sentences were commuted to fifteen years after vigorous protests from Western heads of state and others. Today, two of those arrested are still imprisoned— Yuri Fedorov and Alexei Murzhenko, non-Jews.

1971—In February, a petition seeking the right to emigrate to Israel was signed by more than 1,100 Soviet Jews and sent to the United Nations. In March, 156 Jewish activists went to the Presidium in Moscow and demanded the right to emigrate. Shortly thereafter large-scale Jewish emigration from the U.S.S.R. began.

1972—The Soviet Information Office in Paris was successfully sued by the International League Against Anti-Semitism for spreading "public slander against the Jews" in its French-language bulletin. The bulletin was fined 1,500 French francs and ordered to publish the court's ruling in its next issue.

The U.S.S.R. instituted an education tax on persons seeking to emigrate. The tax, which was as high as 35,000 rubles on the most highly educated (when the average salary was about 2,000 rubles per year), was denounced in the West and dropped by the U.S.S.R. in 1973.

1975—The Soviet Union cancelled the 1972 trade agreement with the United States after Congress limited credits and approved the Jackson-Vanik Amendment linking most-favored-nation status to free emigration. Jewish emigration figures dropped significantly in 1975 and 1976.

1977—Anatoly Scharansky, a Moscow Jewish activist who had sought to emigrate, was arrested and charged with treason. After being held in solitary confinement for sixteen months, he was sentenced to thirteen years' imprisonment. Scharansky was one of a number of Jews jailed on a variety of specious political or economic charges—part of the government policy to harass and intimidate Jewish activists and would-be emigrants.

1979—A record 51,000 Soviet Jews emigrated, superseding the previous record of 34,000 in 1973.

1980—Emigration declined precipitously from the 1979 level as Soviet authorities made it more difficult even to apply for an exit visa. Anti-Semitic incidents increased and uncertainty about the future course of emigration prevailed.

Reprinted by permission from "The Indispensable Guide to Soviet Jewry," by David Geller and David Harris, *Present Tense Magazine*, Autumn, 1980. Copyright 1980, The American Jewish Committee.

6.
Jewish Law and Religion

NINE CRIMES PUNISHABLE BY EXECUTION IN JEWISH LAW

The Bible mentions a total of 36 crimes punishable by execution. Up to the time of the destruction of the Second Temple (70 C.E.), Jewish courts carried out the death sentence for these crimes, though the rigid interrogation of witnesses required to verify that the act actually took place made the death penalty extremely rare. Among the 36 capital offenses are:

1. Cursing one's father or mother
2. Kidnapping
3. Desecrating the Sabbath
4. Zoophilia
5. Idolatry
6. Homosexuality
7. Adultery
8. Murder
9. False prophecy

Ten Questions of Jewish Law Arising from the Holocaust

The scope of halakhah (Jewish law), is so broad as to emcompass any aspect of a Jew's life. Even during the darkest hours of the Holocaust, hundreds of thousands of Jews adhered to the halakhah in all of its detail. The horrifying and unprecedented circumstances they found themselves in gave rise to situations where even the learned Jewish layman found himself ignorant as to the correct course of action. Rabbis in ghettos and concentration camps were called upon to make use of their legal expertise to render decisions. The foremost surviving expert on Holocaust halakhah is Rabbi Ephraim Oshry, who recorded some of the questions he was asked during the Second World War and after in his four-volume *Sheelot u-Teshuvot Mimaamakim (Responsa from the Depths)*. The following is a sample of some of the issues dealt with.

1. May a Jew chance escaping the ghetto of Kovno to join the partisans, at the risk of being killed by Germans if caught escaping, or even by the partisans if he got that far? (Rabbi Oshry encouraged escape attempts as he felt that the risks involved in escaping were no greater than those of staying in the ghetto, and, furthermore, successful escape might give one the opportunity to fulfill the mitzvah [commandment] of fighting the Germans.)

2. Despite the German ban on public prayer, surviving residents of the Kovno ghetto were determined to hold clandestine services on Rosh Hashanah in 1942. The cantor with the best voice was a young man castrated by the Germans. Could he lead the services? (Yes. A eunuch can

serve as a cantor occasionally with the consent of the congregation. He cannot hold a permanent cantorial position.)

3. May one whose left hand had been chopped off by the Germans wear his tefillin (phylacteries) on his right hand? (Yes.)

4. Is there an obligation to hunt Nazi war criminals? (Rabbi Oshry ruled that Jews are obligated to support efforts to bring German war criminals to justice.)

5. After the liberation of Lithuania, two local natives who assisted the Germans in their slaughter of the Jews were found and put on trial. Despite the protestations of the remnants of the local Jewish community, a Jewish lawyer defended the pair. Months later, on the anniversary of the death of one of his parents, the lawyer wanted to lead the prayer service in the synagogue in accordance with Jewish custom. As the lawyer approached the cantor's lectern, he was grabbed by the sexton and forcibly evicted from the synagogue. Was the sexton justified in his action? (Yes, because someone unacceptable to the majority of the congregation has no right to lead services.)

6. May a former concentration camp inmate remove the numbers tattooed on her arm by the Germans by means of plastic surgery? (No. The tattoo should be viewed by Jews as a sign of honor and a testimony to German bestiality.)

7. Is it permitted to re-use clothing worn by people at the time they were shot by the Germans? (The clothing should be given to the heirs of those murdered, who may use them, providing they are not stained with the blood of the deceased. If the clothes are blood-stained they must be buried.)

8. Two families in the ghetto of Kovno were sharing a house. One family was executed by the Germans. May members of the surviving family sell the few possessions left in the house by the other family to keep from starving? (Yes.)
9. Could residents of the ghetto say that part of the prayer service thanking G-d for not making them slaves despite the fact that they were, in the best of circumstances, performing slave labor for the Germans? (Yes. The prayer is one of thanks for freedom of the spirit, rather than freedom from physical bondage.)
10. May one say kaddish (the memorial prayer for the dead) for a Gentile who saved the lives of Jews? (Yes.)

An excellent English book on this topic is *Holocaust and Halakhah*, by Irving J. Rosenbaum, Ktav Publishing House, New York, 1976.

The Five Steps of Jewish Ritual Circumcision

1. THE MOHEL (circumciser) takes hold of the amount of foreskin to be cut off and clamps a metal shield below it to protect the glans penis.
2. CHITTUCH (cutting)—The foreskin is sliced off with a sharp knife.
3. PERIAH (uncovering)—The mucous membrane exposed after the chittuch is torn by the mohel with his fingernails and pushed back behind the glans.
4. METZITZAH (sucking)—The mohel sucks some blood from the wound either directly or through a glass tube and spits it out.

5. Cleaning and bandaging of the wound.

THREE JEWISH FOODS DEVISED TO AVOID VIOLATING JEWISH LAW

1. GEFILTE FISH—One of the food-related activities forbidden on the Sabbath is *borer,* separating that which is inedible from that which is edible. For this reason, Orthodox Jews to this very day, when eating chicken on the Sabbath, will not remove bones from chicken but rather remove the meat of the chicken from the bone. This is easy enough with chicken but not so with fish. In order to have their Shabbos fish and avoid *borer* problems, medieval European Jews invented gefilte fish, with the bones either removed or ground up with the rest of the fish before the onset of the Sabbath.

2. CHOLENT—"On the day of the Sabbath you shall not have a fire burning in any of your settlements." The Sadducees, an ancient Jewish sect, took this Biblical verse literally and had no fire burning in their homes throughout the Sabbath. The Pharisees adhered to the rabbinic tradition that this verse forbade only the igniting of a fire on the Sabbath but permitted a fire ignited before the Sabbath to burn throughout the Sabbath. To prove their point, the Pharisees decreed that Jews must eat hot food at the noon meal on the Sabbath, a tradition widely adhered to, to this very day. This, however, led to another problem, as placing food on a fire to cook or warm is forbidden on the Sabbath. Jewish housewives found a solution, discovering that a stew of meat and starches (beans, potatoes, and barley among Europeans; farina among Orientals) cooked on Friday and allowed to simmer

overnight made a delicious Sabbath meal, and cholent was born.

3. KNISHES—According to Talmudic tradition, one who fills himself with meat without eating bread is considered a glutton. To make sure that no one they cooked for was guilty of gluttony, Jewish housewives put a thin, breadlike, crust around the meat they cooked—thus, the knish.

SEVENTEEN RELATIONSHIPS CONSIDERED INCESTUOUS BY JEWISH LAW

1. Mother and son
2. Grandmother and grandson
3. Stepmother and stepson
4. Step-grandmother and step-grandson
5. Wife of father's or mother's brother and her nephew by marriage
6. Sister and brother
7. Father and daughter
8. Stepfather and stepdaughter
9. Grandfather and granddaughter
10. Step-grandfather and step-granddaughter
11. Mother-in-law and son-in-law (even after death of wife or divorce)
12. Father-in-law and daughter-in-law (even after death of husband or divorce)
13. Grandfather and grandson's wife (even after death of grandson or divorce)
14. Grandmother and granddaughter's husband (even after death of granddaughter or divorce)
15. Brother-in-law and brother's wife (except where brother dies childless)

16. Brother-in-law and wife's sister (permitted after death of wife)
17. Mother or father's sister and nephew (but marriage between uncle and niece is permitted)

SIX MEN WHO KNOW THE TALMUD BY HEART

The Talmud is the primary source of the oral tradition of Jewish law and philosophy. Roughly the size of the *Encyclopaedia Brittanica,* the standard edition of the Talmud with its major commentaries comprises twenty folio volumes. The following men have mastered this massive work to the point that they can quote anywhere from it verbatim.

1. RABBI MOSHE FEINSTEIN—This resident of Manhattan's Lower East Side is the epitome of the Jewish scholar-saint. One of Rabbi Feinstein's acquaintances once remarked, "It's impossible to talk to the man without him making you feel like you're doing him a favor."
2. RABBI OVADIA YOSEF—Sephardic Chief Rabbi of Israel. Rabbi Yosef is known for his remarkable mastery of the responsa, over 2,000 volumes of replies to questions of law written by rabbis over the past twelve centuries.
3. DR. CHAIM ZIMMERMAN—The outspoken Dr. Zimmerman is an expert in the natural and physical sciences, as well as Jewish law and philosophy.
4. RABBI SHLOMO FISHER—Professor of Talmud at Jerusalem's Israel Torah Research Institute, Rabbi Fisher is currently devoting himself to the study of Jewish mysticism.
5. RABBI ISRAEL ZEV GUSTMAN—A prodigy among prewar Lithuanian Jewry, Rabbi Gustman sat on the world's most

prestigious rabbinic court, the *bet din* of Vilna, at the age of 17. He currently resides in Jerusalem, where he heads the Netzach Israel Seminary.

6. DR. SAUL LEIBERMAN—Professor of Talmud at New York's Jewish Theological Seminary, Dr. Leiberman is the author of *Tosefta Kipshuta,* a commentary on one of the more obscure sections of the Talmud. He died in 1983.

THREE CHIEF RABBIS OF THE UNITED STATES

1. RABBI JACOB JOSEPH—A leading Lithuanian scholar, Rabbi Joseph was invited to the chief rabbinate by the growing community on New York's Lower East Side in 1888. A congenial man, with lofty ideals, Rabbi Joseph's lack of fluency in the English language and his overwhelming administrative problems were major factors which contributed to his failure to exercise the authority that might have been expected to accompany his position. His funeral in 1902, attended by tens of thousands, ended in a riot between Jewish and Irish inhabitants of the East Side. Lt. Jacob Joseph, the rabbi's grandson, was the first American to be killed in the Battle of Guadalcanal.

2. RABBI HAIM VIEDROVITZ—A contemporary of Rabbi Joseph, Rabbi Viedrovitz was the spiritual leader of a number of Hasidic congregations. His door displayed a shingle proclaiming him to be Chief Rabbi of America. When asked who appointed him to this position, Rabbi Viedrovitz, whose stutter was as pronounced as his wit, replied, "The p-p-painter."

3. RABBI ELIEZER SILVER—Rabbi Silver of Cincinnati (d. 1965) was the last president of the Union of American Rabbis to use the title of Chief Rabbi, and only rarely at that. The driver

of a car he was riding in, stopped by the police for speeding, protested, "Do you know who that is in the back seat? That's the Chief Rabbi of the United States!" To which Rabbi Silver chimed in, "And Canada."

Sources: (1) Ande Manners, *Poor Cousins;* (2) Judah David Eisenstein, *Autobiography and Memoirs;* (3) popular anecdote.

The Nine Most Powerful Rabbis in New York (as listed in *New York Magazine,* Jan. 22, 1979)

1. RABBI MOSHE FEINSTEIN—Universally acknowledged as the world's greatest authority on Jewish law, Rabbi Feinstein, more than anyone else, shapes the path that Orthodox Jews take in their approach to such modern-day problems as what types of birth control are permissible, whether one may use automatic elevators on the Sabbath, and the like.
2. RABBI ALEXANDER SCHINDLER—President of the Union of American Hebrew Congregations. During his tenure as chairman of the Conference of Presidents of Major American Jewish Organizations, Rabbi Schindler influenced the Carter administration to ease its pressure on the Begin government during mid-East peace negotiations.
3. RABBI MENACHEM SCHNEERSON—The Lubavitcher Rebbe. Spiritual leader of New York's most cohesive and influential Hasidic sect.
4. RABBI MARC H. TANNENBAUM—Director of national interreligious affairs of the American Jewish Committee, Rabbi Tannenbaum is at the forefront of Jewish-Christian dialogue.
5. RABBI SHLOMO RISKIN—The dynamic modern Orthodox rabbi and educator is the driving force behind New York's

fastest-growing Orthodox synagogue and a number of educational institutions.

6. RABBI JOEL TEITELBAUM*—Spiritual leader of the Satmar Hasidim of Williamsburg and Borough Park, New York's largest Hasidic sect.

7. RABBI SEYMOUR SIEGAL—Professor of ethics and theology at the Jewish Theological Seminary.

8. RABBI MORRIS SHERER—President of Agudath Israel of America, a politically influential organization of Orthodox Jews.

9. RABBI ISAAC N. TRAININ—Head of the Department of Religious Affairs of the Federation of Jewish Philanthropies.

*since deceased

Four Sons of Cantors

1. AL JOLSON—born Asa Joelson
2. GEORGE GERSHWIN
3. HOWARD ARLEN—composer of "Somewhere over the Rainbow"
4. EDDIE CANTOR

Source: Irving Howe, *World of Our Fathers.*

Four Shabbos Goyim
(Gentiles hired by Orthodox Jews to perform activities forbidden to Jews on the Sabbath)

1. JOSEPH P. KENNEDY—Father of the illustrious political trio. His first paying job was lighting fires on Saturday for Jews.

2. NIKITA KHRUSHCHEV—In 1913, Khrushchev rented a room with a Jewish family in Mariopol, Russia. In return for acting as Shabbos goy, he would be rewarded with gefilte fish.

3. CHUCK CONNORS—In the TV and film star's own words, "I'm a Shabbos shaigetz from Brooklyn, and I'll be happy to light your fire."

4. PAT COOPER—The Italian comic used to turn off lights for his Jewish landlord in Brooklyn.

Sources: (1) Robert Whalen, *The Founding Father: The Story of Joseph P. Kennedy;* (2) *Jewish Digest,* April 1964; (3) Phil Blazer's column in *Israel Today;* (4) David Fishof's column in the *Jewish Press.*

FOUR UNUSUAL JEWISH PRAYERS

1. The eighteenth century *Siddur Bet Yakov,* compiled by Rabbi Jacob Emden, contains a blessing to be recited before being murdered by non-Jews for religious reasons.

2. The 1957 Soviet edition of the Jewish prayerbook, one of the last printed in that country, contains the following prayer:
   May He who blessed our fathers Abraham, Isaac, and Jacob, He who makes pathways in the mighty seas, bless, guard, aid, glorify, and exalt the government of the Union of Soviet Socialist Republics. May the Holy One, blessed be He, give it life, guard it, and save it from any trouble, oppression, anguish, and damage. May He cause its enemies to fall, and may it succeed in all that it endeavors. Let us say Amen.

3. Isaac Mayer Wise, father of American Reform Judaism, in the first edition of his *Union Prayer Book,* carries an English translation of the daily prayer *"La-Kel Baruch"* ("To the

blessed G-d") containing the unfamiliar phrase "arm of justice." Wise confused the Hebrew word *zorea* (sower) with
zeroa (arm). Subsequent editions contain the correct
phrase, "sower of justice."

4. A prayer composed by concentration camp inmates upon
having to eat leavened bread on Passover:

"Our Father in heaven, it is known and revealed before
You that it is Your will and our will to celebrate the holiday of
Passover by eating matzoh and not violating the prohibition
against eating leavened bread. On account of this our hearts
are saddened—that our thralldom prevents us [from eating
matzoh], and we are in danger of death. Behold we are ready
to fulfill Your commandment of "You shall live by them [the
commandments] and not die by them," and to carefully obey
the warning, "Take care and guard your life very much."
Therefore it is our prayer to You that You sustain and
preserve us so that we may observe Your laws and perform
Your will and serve You wholeheartedly, Amen."

MENACHEM BEGIN'S LIST OF MOST INSPIRING JEWISH RELIGIOUS FIGURES

This list was graciously contributed by Mr. Begin, but the
comments in parentheses are not the Prime Minister's.

1. MOSES
2. NACHMANIDES—(Thirteenth-century Spanish rabbi. He emigrated to Jerusalem toward the end of his life, where he
reinvigorated the dwindling Jewish community.)
3. RABBI ELIJAH OF VILNA—(Known as the "Genius of Vilna,"
this eighteenth-century rabbi is universally acknowledged to
be the greatest Jewish thinker of the past 500 years.)

4. RABBI ARYEH LEVIN—(This Palestinian rabbi was known for his self-sacrifice in tending to the needs of Jewish political prisoners during the period of the British Mandate.)
5. RABBI ISAAC ZEV SOLOVEICHIK—(Chief Rabbi of Mr. Begin's hometown of Brisk, Lithuania, and one of the great Talmudists of last generation, Rabbi Soloveichik [uncle of Rabbi Joseph B. Soloveichik of Boston] emigrated to Palestine during World War II. Possessed of a brilliant mathematical mind, he was known for his strict observance of the minutiae of Jewish law, uncompromising adherence to his principles, and, ironically, staunch anti-Zionism.)

FOUR EX-COMMUNICANTS

The Talmud lists twenty-four offenses punishable by excommunication (exclusion from the Jewish community), but it has most commonly been applied in instances of heresy or egregious rejection of rabbinic authority.

1. BARUCH SPINOZA—Excommunicated in 1656 for espousing views deemed heretical, such as disbelief in the divine origin of the Bible.
2. THE SEDER GUEST—A nineteenth-century Hungarian Jew excommunicated one of the guests at his Passover seder for scoffing at the *Chad Gadya* song as being no more than a nursery rhyme. Rabbi Moshe Sofer, leading rabbinic authority of the period, upheld the ban.
3. MORDECHAI KAPLAN—The American rabbinate has imposed excommunication only once in its history, in 1945, against Mordechai Kaplan, founder of the Reconstructionist movement in Judaism.
4. SHLOMO LORINCZ—The Chief Rabbinate Council of Israel

excommunicated the Knesset member for comparing Chief Rabbi Shlomo Goren to Idi Amin.

SEVEN EVENTS THAT TOOK PLACE ON THE NINTH OF AV

The saddest day of the Jewish calendar, Tishah b'Av (the Ninth of Av) occurs in July or August of the solar year. Tradition holds that the following tragedies took place on that day:

1. The decree that those Jews who left Egypt should die in the desert and not enter the Land of Israel
2. The destruction of the First Temple
3. The destruction of the Second Temple
4. The capture of Betar, last stronghold of Bar Kochba's army, by the Romans in 135 C.E.
5. The establishment of a pagan temple on Jerusalem's Temple Mount in 136 C.E.
6. The Crusaders' conquest of Jerusalem in 1099. On that day, the Crusaders locked the entire Jewish population of Jerusalem into their synagogue and burned the building down, killing all inside.
7. The expulsion of the Jews from Spain in 1492.

And here's a remarkable coincidence. On February 21, 1973, at 2:07 P.M., Israeli Air Force jets downed a Libyan airliner which strayed over the Sinai Peninsula when it failed to identify itself, killing most of the passengers on board. On February 21, 1970, at 2:07 P.M., the pilot of a Swissair airliner bound for Israel announced over the radio that an explosion had gone off in his plane and that he was going to crash. Palestinian terrorists claimed responsibility for the incident, which took the lives of all 47 on board.

MAIMONIDES' EIGHT LEVELS OF CHARITY

1. The highest level of charity is giving a fellow Jew a gift, a loan, or a job so that he can become financially independent.
2. The next level is giving to the poor in such a way that the benefactor does not know the identity of the recipient nor the recipient that of the benefactor.
3. Next is where the benefactor knows the identity of the recipient but the recipient does not know the benefactor.
4. Following comes the level where the recipient knows the benefactor but the benefactor does not know the recipient.
5. Giving money directly to a poor person before he asks is the next level.
6. Giving after the poor person asks is lower.
7. Giving less than the proper sum, but cheerfully, is the next level.
8. Giving begrudgingly is the lowest level.

7.

Show Biz

THE TWENTY-NINE MOST POPULAR JEWISH MOVIES OF ALL TIME

The following is a list of the most popular movies to prominently feature Jewish characters. Figures indicate rental fees paid to the distributor, not ticket sales, as they appeared in the January 14, 1981, issue of *Variety*.*

1. BLAZING SADDLES $45,300,000
2. THE TEN COMMANDMENTS 43,000,000
3. FIDDLER ON THE ROOF 40,500,000
4. BEN HUR (1959) 36,650,000
5. PRIVATE BENJAMIN 34,000,000
6. THE WAY WE WERE 25,000,000
7. CABARET 20,250,000
8. ANNIE HALL 18,100,000
9. MANHATTAN 17,000,000
10. MARATHON MAN 16,575,000
11. THE BIBLE 15,000,000
12. BLACK SUNDAY 14,202,000
13. JESUS CHRIST SUPERSTAR 13,291,000

14. JULIA 13,055,000
15. SAMSON AND DELILAH 11,500,000
16. NORMA RAE 11,413,000
17. GOODBYE COLUMBUS................... 10,500,000
18. THE BOYS FROM BRAZIL 10,165,000
19. THE LIFE OF BRIAN 10,100,000
20. EXODUS 8,320,000
21. THE JOLSON STORY 7,600,000
22. WHOLLY MOSES........................ 7,527,000
23. THE HEARTBREAK KID 5,530,000
24. IT'S MY TURN 5,515,000
25. THE FRISCO KID 5,200,000
26. SOLOMON AND SHEBA 5,200,000
27. JOLSON SINGS AGAIN 5,000,000
28. DAVID AND BATHSHEBA 4,720,000
29. BEN HUR (1926) 4,000,000

*Reprinted with permission. Copyright 1981. Variety, Inc.

FIVE JEWISH ACTORS WHO PLAYED NAZIS IN THE MOVIES

1. LUDWIG DONATH
2. MARTIN KOSLECK
3. OTTO PREMINGER
4. CONRAD VEIDT
5. ERICH VON STROHEIM

LEO ROSTEN ON THE GREATEST JEWISH HUMORISTS OF ALL TIME

The first humorist I ever encountered was Sholem Aleichem.

My father used to read me his incomparable tales in Yiddish from the *Forvertz* (*Jewish Daily Forward*), from the time I was five years old. I've not since, having read his collected tales, found a humorist to compare with him save one: Mark Twain.

It is not wit that distinguishes Sholem Aleichem, though he was very witty indeed. It is the marvelous characterizations, the compassion for human types, the exquisite ruminations, the wry, dry turn of mind—and the underlying sense of sadness, of pathos, that runs through his work as music. His satire and mischief endow him with an altogether unique resonance (as a physicist might say).

I place "Mendele" (Seforim) in the top rank of writers, no less than humorists. He does not perhaps translate as vividly as Aleichem. American humor, from the days of vaudeville on, owes an enormous debt to American Jewish writers. In books, plays, movies, popular song and—emphatically—television, the special stance of Jewish humor is ubiquitous.

S. J. Perelman stands alone for sheer wizardry of the English language deployed for mockery. George Kaufman, alone or with Moss Hart, brought a new style of comedy to the American and English stage. Al Capp was an authentic Jewish original: "Li'l Abner" and his unforgettable cohorts (their names alone trigger laughter) are parts of national folklore. Neil Simon and his one-line boffs have set him apart as a playwright and movie author. Woody Allen has picked up the magic of Charlie Chaplin, Harry Langdon, and Stan Laurel to give us an apotheosis of the shlemiel.

The list of Jewish comedians is so long as to be mind-boggling. Smith and Dale introduced the risible uses of English to American vaudeville, and their special wit influenced countless writers after them. Groucho Marx is, of course, *sui generis,* as were Chico and Harpo. The Marx Brothers comedy began with the Jewish writers who forged their hilarious dialogue (Kaufman, Morrie Ryskind, *et alia*). But in his own right, Groucho was a superlative wit. ("From the moment I picked this book up until the moment I put it down, I could not stop laughing. Some day I hope to read it.")

One must pay tribute to the individual style of Jack Benny, the glorious *nebich*. As an after-dinner speaker, George Jessel developed a manner few could imitate. George Burns remains a master of the throw-away line.

I must pay particular tribute to the writers of television's crowning comedies: the writers of the *Mary Tyler Moore Show, All in the Family* (superbly overseen by Norman Lear), and *M*A*S*H*.

In the theater, the priceless comedic sense of Frank Loesser (and Abe Burrows) gleams undiminished by time.

Movie writers are generally not known much outside of Hollywood, but I would call attention to those who wrote the durable films of Bob Hope and Bing Crosby, some of the Cary Grant comedies, the Danny Kaye films, the vehicles for Walter Matthau.

I have not mentioned Jewish short-story writers and novelists, for their number, if not their name, is legion.

ONE HUNDRED AND THREE JEWISH COMEDIANS AND HUMORISTS

1. DON ADAMS
2. MARTY ALLEN
3. WOODY ALLEN
4. MOREY AMSTERDAM
5. BEA ARTHUR
6. SANDY BARON
7. RICHARD BELZER
8. JACK BENNY
9. DAVE BERG
10. MILTON BERLE

11. SHELLEY BERMAN
12. JOEY BISHOP
13. DAVID BRENNER
14. MARSHALL BRICKMAN
15. MEL BROOKS
16. LENNY BRUCE
17. ART BUCHWALD
18. GEORGE BURNS
19. RED BUTTONS
20. SID CAESAR
21. EDDIE CANTOR
22. AL CAPP
23. JACK CARTER
24. CHARLIE CHAPLIN
25. MYRON COHEN
26. "PROFESSOR" IRWIN COREY
27. NORM CROSBY
28. CURLY
29. BILL DANA
30. RODNEY DANGERFIELD
31. JACK EAGLE
32. JULES FEIFFER
33. MARTY FELDMAN
34. ALBERT FELDSTEIN
35. TOTIE FIELDS
36. PHIL FOSTER
37. DAVID FRYE
38. JACKIE GAYLE
39. MORTY GUNTY
40. JACK GILFORD
41. HAL GOODMAN
42. SHECKY GREEN
43. BUDDY HACKETT

44. VAN HARRIS
45. GOLDIE HAWN
46. JOSEPH HELLER
47. STANLEY MYRON HENDELMAN
48. MARTY INGELS
49. GEORGE JESSEL
50. MADELINE KAHN
51. MILT KAMEN
52. GABE KAPLAN
53. ANDY KAUFMAN
54. DANNY KAYE
55. ALAN KING
56. ROBERT KLEIN
57. BERT LAHR
58. LARRY
59. LOUISE LASSER
60. FRAN LEIBOWITZ
61. HARVEY LEMBECK
62. JACK E. LEONARD
63. SAM LEVENSON
64. GREG LEWIS
65. JERRY LEWIS
66. SHARI LEWIS
67. MARCEL MARCEAU
68. STEVE MARTIN
69. CHICO MARX
70. GROUCHO MARX
71. HARPO MARX
72. ELAINE MAY
73. MOE
74. HENRY MORGAN
75. JAN MURRAY

76. MIKE NICHOLS
77. LOUIS NYE
78. S. J. PERELMAN
79. MARTHA RAYE
80. CARL REINER
81. ROB REINER
82. DON RICKLES
83. JOAN RIVERS
84. LEO ROSTEN
85. PHILIP ROTH
86. MORT SAHL
87. SOUPY SALES
88. PETER SELLERS
89. DICK SHAWN
90. SHEMP
91. ALAN SHERMAN
92. FRANK SHUSTER
93. PHIL SILVERS
94. NEIL SIMON
95. DAVID STEINBERG
96. SOL STEINBERG
97. STUIE STONE
98. LARRY STORCH
99. JOHNNY WAYNE
100. GENE WILDER
101. HENRY WINKLER
102. ED WYNN
103. HENNY YOUNGMAN

THREE JEWISH CREW MEMBERS OF STARSHIP *ENTERPRISE*

1. MR. SPOCK—Leonard Nimoy
2. CAPTAIN KIRK—William Shatner
3. ENSIGN PAVEL CHEKHOV—Walter Koenig

SIX JEWS WHO'VE STARRED AS TV DETECTIVES

1. PETER FALK—*Columbo*
2. JACK LORD—*Hawaii 5-0*
3. BARRY NEWMAN—*Petrocelli*
4. JESSICA WALTERS—*Amy Prentiss*
5. PAUL MICHAEL GLASER—*Starsky and Hutch*
6. GENE BARRY—*Amos Burke*

TV SERIES WITH JEWISH THEMES

1. THE GOLDBERGS—A popular fifties comedy about a European Jewish family living in New York.
2. MRS. G. GOES TO COLLEGE—A 1961 spin-off from *The Goldbergs*.
3. THE LAW—The hero of this three-week NBC mini-series was a Jewish lawyer, Murray Stone, played by a Jewish actor, Judd Hirsh.
4. BRIDGET LOVES BERNIE—A short-lived 1972 comedy about a Catholic woman married to a Jewish man. Canceled amid loud protests over its appearance by the Jewish community and because of low ratings.
5. RHODA—When this Jewish New York career girl married a Gentile on her series a few years later, few complaints were heard.
6. HOLOCAUST—This 1978 mini-series was one of the most popular shows ever screened.

TEN JEWS WHO WON OSCARS FOR BEST ACTOR OR ACTRESS

1. NORMA SHEARER—1929, *The Divorcee*
2. FREDERIC MARCH—1932, *Dr. Jekyll and Mr. Hyde,* and 1946, *The Best Years of Our Lives*
3. LUISE RAINER—1936, *The Great Ziegfield,* and 1937, *The Good Earth.*
4. PAUL MUNI—1936, *The Story of Louis Pasteur*
5. JUDY HOLLIDAY—1950, *Born Yesterday*
6. SIMONE SIGNORET—1959, *Room at the Top*

7. ELIZABETH TAYLOR—1961, *Butterfield 8,* and 1966, *Who's Afraid of Virginia Woolfe?*
8. BARBRA STREISAND—1968, *Funny Girl*
9. RICHARD DREYFUSS—1977, *The Goodbye Girl*
10. DUSTIN HOFFMAN—1979, *Kramer vs. Kramer*

Meryl Streep who played opposite Hoffman in *Kramer vs. Kramer* and won the Academy Award for Best Supporting Actress is also of Jewish ancestry. She won the 1982 Academy Award for Best Actress for *Sophie's Choice.*

YIDL MIT A FENDER
Jews and Judaism in Modern Popular Music

PART ONE
A DICTIONARY OF JEWS IN ROCK, POP, FOLK, SOUL, AND COUNTRY

HERB ABRAMSON—One of the founders of Atlantic Records and an important early rock producer.

HERB ALPERT—President of A & M Records and America's most popular trumpeter.

ALAN ARKIN—Better known as an actor, Arkin was a top folk-singer in the '50s, both as a solo performer and with his group, the Tarriers.

IRVING AZOFF—Rock music's top agent, representing the Eagles, Boz Scaggs, Steely Dan, Warren Zevon, and many more.

MARTY BALIN (Martyn Jarel Buchwald)—One of the leading figures in the Jefferson Airplane, now a solo performer. There is a persistent rumor that he is Jewish.

JEFF BARRY (Adelberg)—Composer of "Sugar, Sugar," "Tell

Laura I Love Her," "River Deep, Mountain High," and many more rock hits.

PAUL BERNSTEIN—Bass guitarist with the Cretones.

SID BERNSTEIN—He managed the Young Rascals and brought the Beatles to America.

ALAN BETROCK—Founder and former editor of *New York Rocker.*

JAY BLACK—Jay of Jay and the Americans. He's a graduate of Manhattan Talmudic Academy.

ERIC BLOOM—Guitarist with the Blue Oyster Cult.

MIKE BLOOMFIELD—A talented blues guitarist, he rose to the height of his popularity in the late 60s with his band The Electric Flag. As his career declined, Bloomfield was reduced to doing soundtracks for pornographic movies. He died in February 1981 of a possible drug overdose, at the age of 37.

DAVE BLUE (David Cohen)—Greenwich Village folksinger popular in the 60s.

ROY BLUMENFELD—Bass guitarist with the Blues Project, a mid-60s New York group way ahead of its time.

NEIL BOGART (Bogatz)-Former president of Casablanca Records, now head of Boardwalk Entertainment Company.

MARC BOLAN (Feld)—Singer with the British group T. Rex. He died in an automobile accident in 1977 at the age of 29. Bolan was a graduate of London's Jewish Free School.

KARLA BONOFF—Singer-songwriter who wrote Linda Ronstadt's "Hasten Down the Wind."

JOHN BOWZER (Bauman)—Pianist with Sha Na Na.

BRUCE BRODY—Pianist who has backed Patti Smith and John Cale. Currently with VHF.

DAVE BROMBERG—A versatile performer, proficient in several instruments and musical genres. One of Bob Dylan's favorites.

STEVE BRONSTEIN—A member of Elephant's Memory, a New York group that had a hit in 1970 with "Mongoose" and played on the soundtrack of *Midnight Cowboy*.

ELKIE BROOKS (Elaine Bookbinder)—British blues singer.

LEE BROVITZ—Bass guitarist with Blue Angel.

ELLIOT CAHN—Guitarist and vocalist with Sha Na Na.

RANDY CALIFORNIA—Guitarist with Spirit.

ALLAN CARR (Solomon)—Producer of the film version of *Sergeant Pepper's Lonely Hearts' Club Band*.

DAVID COHEN—Lead guitarist with Country Joe and the Fish.

JOHN COHEN—Singer with the New Lost City Ramblers, popular '50s and '60s folk music group.

LEONARD COHEN—Canadian poet, singer, songwriter.

NICK COHN—Top British rock critic.

MORT COOPERMAN—Manager of the Lone Star Cafe, New York's top country-music club.

DICK DALE—An early performer of surf music who had a couple of hits in the early '60s.

CLIVE DAVIS—President of Arista Records.

RON DELSENER—Owner of the Palladium. Currently the biggest rock promoter in New York.

MAGIC DICK (Richard Salwitz)—Blues-harp player with the J. Geils Band.

NEIL DIAMOND—Composer and singer turned actor in the remake of Al Jolson's *The Jazz Singer*.

STEVE DIOR (Hershkowitz)—Guitarist with the Idols who also backed the late Sid Vicious during his short-lived career as a solo performer.

BOB DYLAN (Robert Allen Zimmerman)—The personification of the ultimate musical superstar.

LINDA EASTMAN—Mrs. Paul McCartney. Keyboards player with Wings.

SHERMAN EDWARDS—Composer of "Johnny Get Angry," "Wonderful, Wonderful," "See You in September," and other pop hits of the 60s.

CASS ELLIOT (Ellen Naomi Cohen)—"Mama Cass" of the Mamas and Papas.

RAMBLIN' JACK ELLIOTT (Elliott Adnopoz)—A protegé of Woody Guthrie and one of America's most popular folksingers for over a quarter of a century.

BRIAN EPSTEIN—Manager who led the Beatles to stardom.

DOUG FEIGER—Vocalist, guitarist with the Knack. His "Sharona" is Sharona Alperin, a graduate of a Los Angeles Jewish School.

ROBERT FELDMAN—One of the Strangeloves, a group that had one hit in 1965, "I Want Candy."

RICHIE FLEIGLER—Back-up guitarist for John Cale, Lou Reed, and Genya Ravan, among others. Currently with VHF.

DANNY FRANKEL—Drummer for the Urban Verbs.

DAVID FREIBERG—Bass guitarist with the Quicksilver Messenger Service and Jefferson Starship.

MARTY FRIED—Drummer with the Cyrkle, a group managed by Brian Epstein which had two hits in 1966, "Red Rubber Ball" (written by Paul Simon) and "Turn Down Day."

DAVID FRIEDMAN—Drummer with Double Image.

KINKY FRIEDMAN—First (and only) performer of Jewish country music, with his group the Texas Jewboys.

MARTIN FULTERMAN—A member of the New York Rock Ensemble, a band of classically trained musicians which enjoyed modest success in the early 70s.

SHELLEY GANZ—Singer/guitarist with the Unclaimed, contemporary L.A. new-wave band.

ART GARFUNKLE—One half of Simon and Garfunkle.

DAVID GEFFEN—President of Geffen Records.

DAVID GETZ—Drummer with Big Brother and the Holding Company.

TONY GIBBER—British singer, with a few singles to his credit.

PHILIP GLASS—A composer and performer of experimental electronic music, whose work has strongly influenced a number of avant-garde rock bands.

GERRY GOFFIN—With co-writer (and wife) Carole King, he penned many of the hit tunes of the late 50s and early 60s.

LOUISE GOFFIN—Daughter of Carole King and Gerry Goffin. Her debut album, *Kid Blue*, was released in 1979.

BARRY GOLDBERG—Organist with the Paul Butterfield Blues Band.

MARK GOLDENBERG—Guitarist with the Cretones.

HARVEY GOLDSTEIN—Bass guitarist on Bob Dylan's *Highway 61 Revisited* album.

JERRY GOLDSTEIN—One of the Strangeloves (see ROBERT FELDMAN).

RICHARD GOLDSTEIN—One of the earliest serious critics of rock music and the first to have a volume of his reviews and articles published (*Goldstein's Greatest Hits*, in 1970).

ROBERT GOLDSTEIN—Guitarist with the Urban Verbs.

JERRY GOODMAN—Violinist with John McGlaughlin's Mahavishnu Orchestra.

STEVE GOODMAN—A fine country singer and songwriter.

LESLEY GORE—"It's My Party," which hit number one in the spring of 1963, was the first of her string of hits.

LOU GOTTLEIB—A Ph.D. in musicology, Gottleib was bassist with the Limeliters, a folk group popular in the early 60s.

BILL GRAHAM (Wolfgang Grajonca)—No, not the preacher, but one of the foremost enterpreneurs in rock, founder of the Fillmore, and manager of Santana. Graham was raised by Jewish foster parents in Brooklyn. I don't know if his natural parents were Jewish or if he is a convert, but he does refer to himself as a Jew.

PETER GREEN (Greenbaum)—Original lead guitarist with Fleetwood Mac and one of the finest blues-rockers of the 60s. He has recently started a solo career after an eight-year retirement from the music business.

NORMAN GREENBAUM—Had a smash hit in 1971 with "Spirit in the Sky" (in which he repeats the line "I've got a friend in Jesus" no less than four times). Greenbaum sank into obscurity after his next record, "Canned Ham," flopped.

JERRY GREENBERG—President of Atlantic Records.

PETER GREENBERG—Lead guitarist with Boston band, DMZ.

STEVEN GREENBERG—Wrote "Funkytown," a number-one hit for Lipps, Inc., in the summer of 1980.

ALBERT GROSSMAN—Manager who brought Bob Dylan, The Band, and Peter, Paul, and Mary to stardom.

ARLO GUTHRIE—Son of Woody Guthrie and his Jewish wife Marjorie Mazia. His classic song is "Alice's Restaurant."

MARVIN HAMLISCH—Had a number-one hit in 1974 with his rendition of "The Entertainer," theme song from the motion picture *The Sting*.

RICHARD HELL (Myers)—Leader of Richard Hell and the Voidoids, punk-rock band.

CHICKEN HIRSH—Drummer with Country Joe and the Fish.

JERRY HYMAN—Trombonist with Blood, Sweat, and Tears.

MITCH HYMAN—Guitarist with the Rattlers (and Joey Ramone's brother).

JANIS IAN (Fink)—Hit the top of the charts in 1967 with "Society's Child," a song about interracial dating, when she was just fifteen. Still a very popular performer.

MICK JAGGER—According to *Big Fat Magazine*, a rock publication from Ann Arbor, Michigan, which lasted for three issues in 1970, Jagger's mother, Eve, was a Yemenite Jew. If true, that would make him a member of the tribe.

BILLY JOEL—A singer who spans middle-of-road and rock and roll.

BARRY JONES—A black English Jew who plays guitar with the Idols.

SHEL KAGAN—Producer of some of the Velvet Underground's best material.

MICHAEL KAMEN—A member of the New York Rock Ensemble (see MARTIN FULTERMAN).

DAVID KAPRALIK—Manager who brought Sly and the Family Stone to stardom.

NATASHA KAPUSTIN—A member of Black Russian, the first Russian emigré rock group.

SERGEI KAPUSTIN—Another member of Black Russian.

GARY KATZ—Producer for Steely Dan.

STEVE KATZ—Guitarist with Blood, Sweat, and Tears, and the Blues Project.

MURRAY KAUFMAN—As America's top disc jockey, "Murray the K" was New York's leading rock figure in the '60s.

HOWARD KAYLAN—One of the Turtles. Half of Flo and Edie.

DAVID KERSHENBAUM—Producer for Cat Stevens, Joe Jackson, and other artists who record for A & M Records, where he is vice-president.

CAROLE KING (Carol Klein)—Started as a songwriter for Neil Sedaka and others and is now a superstar singer in her own right.

ALLEN KLEIN—Business manager, at one time or another, for both the Rolling Stones and the Beatles.

DANIEL KLEIN—Bass guitarist with the J. Geils Band.

MARK KNOPFLER—Singer, songwriter, and guitar virtuoso with Dire Straits. Many people say they think he's Jewish, but that might just be due to his Jewish-sounding name.

AL KOOPER—One of rock's most successful producers and a fine musician in his own right, as evidenced by his performance on the *Super Session* album. He was a member of the band that backed Bob Dylan when he recorded "Like a Rolling Stone," along with Mike Bloomfield.

TULI KUPFERBERG—Singer and songwriter with the Fugs, a mildly obscene and intensely funny New York group, popular in the late '60s.

DAVID LANDAU—Lead guitarist in Warren Zevon's band. He also played with Caroline Mas.

JON LANDAU—A onetime prominent rock critic who turned to producing. He did some of the tracks on Bruce Springsteen's *The River*. The people at *Rolling Stone*, where he was once associate editor, think he's Jewish.

LUCKY LEHRER—One of the top drummers on the Los Angeles punk rock scene.

JERRY LEIBER—He and Mike Stoller wrote "Hound Dog," "Kansas City," "There Goes My Baby," and many other early rock hits. More recently they composed material for Stealer's Wheel, whose lead singer was Gerry Rafferty.

ANNIE LEIBOVITZ—A top rock photographer.

DANNY LEVIN—Fiddler with Asleep at the Wheel.

DRAKE LEVIN—Lead guitarist with Paul Revere and the Raiders.

TONY LEVIN—Bass guitarist with Peter Gabriel's band, also appeared on John and Yoko's *Double Fantasy*.

IRWIN LEVINE—Composer (along with L. Russell Brown) of "Tie a Yellow Ribbon Round the Old Oak Tree."

KEITH LEVINE—Guitarist for Public Image, Ltd., the group led by Johnny Lydon (formerly Johnny Rotten of the Sex Pistols).

LARRY LEVINE—Engineer on many of the hits produced by Phil Spector.

MELISSA MANCHESTER—Songstress who topped the charts with "Torn Between Two Lovers" and other hits.

HARVEY MANDEL—Guitarist with Canned Heat.

BARRY MANILOW—Started as a songwriter for Bette Midler.

Now a singer himself, his biggest smashes are "Mandy," "I Write the Songs," and "Copacabana."

MANFRED MANN (Mike Leibovitz)—British organist who has fronted bands named after himself with varying degrees of success since 1964.

KENNY MARGOLIS—Played keyboards and accordion on Mink De Ville's *Le Chat Bleu* album.

ROY MARKOWITZ—Drummer for Main Squeeze and the Kozmic Blues Band, two of the groups that backed Janis Joplin after her break with Big Brother and the Holding Company.

CAROLYNE MAS—New York singer.

DAVID MERRILL—Bass guitarist with the Rattlers (son of opera star Robert Merrill).

BETTE MIDLER—The queen of camp, she won an Academy Award nomination for Best Actress for her role in *The Rose*.

ROD MORGENSTERN—Drummer with the Dixie Dregs.

DOROTHY MOSKOWITZ—Lead vocalist with the United States of America, whose 1968 album of avant-garde music met with critical acclaim but was a commercial flop.

JON MOSS—Percussionist with Culture Club.

RANDY NEWMAN—A singer and songwriter with a strong following. One of his bigger hits is "I Think It's Gonna Rain Today."

LAURA NYRO—Daughter of an Italian father and a Jewish mother. Once one of rock's top singer-songwriters.

PHIL OCHS—A talented folksinger whose career was eclipsed by Bob Dylan. He committed suicide by hanging in 1976, at the age of 35.

SANDY PEARLMAN—Producer for the Clash and the Blue Oyster Cult.

CHUCK PLOTKIN—Producer for Harry Chapin and Andrew Gold.

DOC POMUS—Composer, along with Mort Shuman, of "Young Blood," "Save the Last Dance for Me," "Can't Get Used to Losing You," and a host of other hits.

BUD PRAGER—Manager of Foreigner.

JOEY RAMONE (Jeffrey Hyman)—Singer and guitarist with the Ramones.

GENYA RAVAN (Goldie Zelkowitz)—Born in the pre-Holocaust ghetto of Lodz, Poland, Genya was lead singer for Goldie and the Gingerbreads in the '50s, and lead vocalist for Ten Wheel Drive in the late '60s and early '70s before embarking on a solo career.

HELEN REDDY—Converted to Judaism before marrying her agent, Jeff Wald.

JOSHUA RIFKIN—An associate professor of music at Brandeis University. His recordings of ragtime music were popular in the '70s as a result of the ragtime vogue set off by the motion picture *The Sting*.

IRA ROBBINS—Founder and publisher of *Trouser Press*.

LARRY ROSEN—One of the owners of GRP Records.

RICHIE ROSENBERG—Trombonist for Southside Johnny and the Asbury Jukes.

DAVID LEE ROTH—Guitarist with Van Halen, active in Jewish youth organizations before his rise to stardom.

PAUL ROTHSCHILD—Produced classic albums by the Doors and by Love in the late '60s.

STEVE RUBELL—Co-owner of Studio 54, New York's top disco.

TEX RUBINOWITZ—Washington, D.C., rockabilly star.

DORIAN RUDNYTSKY—A member of the New York Rock Ensemble (see MARTIN FULTERMAN).

BUDDY SALTZMAN—Drummer who backed the Four Seasons on many of their hit recordings.

DAVE SAMUELS—Percussionist with Double Image and Spyrogyra.

SID SCHEINBERG—President of MCA Records.

VLADIMIR SCHNEIDERMAN—A member of Black Russian (see NATASHA KAPUSTIN).

TRACY SCHWARZ—Singer and guitarist with the New Lost City Ramblers (see JOHN COHEN).

NEIL SEDAKA—A product of Flatbush's community of Sephardic Jews.

BRAD SHAPIRO—Producer of some of James Brown's albums.

LEE SHAPIRO—Pianist for the Four Seasons.

MICHAEL SHAPIRO—A member of Elephant's Memory (see STEVE BRONSTEIN).

PETER SHAPIRO—Lead guitarist with Loading Zone, a San Francisco band that had some success after the Jefferson Airplane and Grateful Dead but never went too far. They recorded one album in 1968.

ELLEN SHIPLEY (Schippelkopf)—Brooklyn-born vocalist.

MORT SHUMAN—(See DOC POMUS)

JANIS SEIGEL—Singer with the Manhattan Transfer.

JAY SIEGEL—One of the Tokens. Originally Neil Sedaka's backup group, they had hits of their own in the early 60s, including "The Lion Sleeps Tonight."

SHEL SILVERSTEIN—Composer of country music whose work was prominently featured on Bobby Bare's recent album, *Down and Dirty.*

GENE SIMMONS (Klein)—Bass guitarist with Kiss. The only Israeli-born performer on this list.

PAUL SIMON—The other half of Simon and Garfunkle, his recent hits include "Kodachrome."

FRED SMITH (Lefkowitz)—Bass guitarist with Television, one of the first and best new-wave bands. Not to be confused with Fred "Sonic" Smith, formerly of the MC5, who recently married Patti Smith.

PHOEBE SNOW (Laub)—Jazz and blues singer who has made forays into rock.

LEWIS SOLOFF—Trumpeter with Blood, Sweat, and Tears. He recently appeared on Gil Evans's *Little Wing* album.

MAYNARD SOLOMON—President of Vanguard Records.

PHIL SPECTOR—One of rock's greatest producers. He's worked through the years with such groups as the Ronettes, the Righteous Brothers, and, recently, the Ramones.

PAUL STANLEY (Stanley Eisen)—Guitarist and singer with Kiss.

JEREMY STEIG—Flutist who pioneered in jazz-rock with his group, the Satyrs.

ANDREW STEIN—Saxophonist with Commander Cody and His Lost Planet Airmen.

MARK STEIN—Played keyboards for Vanilla Fudge.

SEYMOUR STEIN—Managing director of Sire Records. He coined the term "new wave," as applied to rock.

JIM STEINMAN—Started out as a songwriter for Meat Loaf, now a performer in his own right. He contributes to Jewish causes, including Esther Jungreis' *Hineni* organization.

MIKE STOLLER—(See JERRY LEIBER).

BARBRA STREISAND—A song stylist and Academy Award-winning actress, her hits include "People," "Second Hand Rose," and "The Way We Were."

RICHARD SUSSMAN—One of the members of Elephant's Memory (see STEVE BRONSTEIN).

RACHEL SWEET—Akron, Ohio, high school student discovered by Stiff Records.

NAT TARNOPOL—Owner of Brunswick Records, a leading force in soul music in the '60s.

RICHARD TEETER—Drummer with the Dictators and VHF.

MARTY THAU—Former manager of the New York Dolls. President of Red Star Records.

MARK VOLMAN—One of the Turtles. The other half of Flo and Eddie.

JEFF WALD—A leading agent for rock performers.

PAUL WASSERMAN—Press agent for James Taylor, Linda Ronstadt, and the Rolling Stones.

CYNTHIA WEIL—Composer, along with Barry Mann, of "Uptown," "You've Lost That Loving Feeling," "We Gotta Get out of This Place," and dozens of other rock classics.

MAX WEINBERG—Drummer with Bruce Springsteen's E Street Band.

TIM WEISBERG—A songwriter and singer with eight albums out by late 1981, his biggest so far, a platinum album, is *Twin Sons from Different Mothers,* done with Dan Fogeberg.

RONNIE WEISER—An Italian Jew who developed a passion for rockabilly music. He came to the States and founded Rolling Rock Records, a leader in the genre.

BEN WEISMAN—Composer of many Elvis Presley hits.

NAT WEISS—President of Nemperor Records.

LESLIE WEST (Weinstein)—One of the most popular guitarists of the '70s, with Mountain and other groups.

JERRY WEXLER—An executive at Warner Brothers Records and one of rock's top producers. He recently did Bob Dylan's *Saved* album.

ELLEN WILLIS—A top rock critic whose work appears in *New Yorker, Rolling Stone,* and other publications.

PETER WOLF (Blankenfield)—Lead singer with the J. Geils Band.

ERIC WOOLFSON—Composer and producer for British avant-garde bands. Recently collaborated with Alan Parsons on a musical version of Edgar Allan Poe's *Tales of Mystery and Imagination.*

ZALMAN YANOVSKY—Guitarist with the Lovin' Spoonful mid-'60s folk-rock sensation.

PETER YARROW—He announced he's Jewish at Peter, Paul, and Mary's June 1983 concert in Jerusalem.

MAX YASGUR—His farm was the site of the Woodstock Rock Festival.

MOSHE YESS—A former sessions musician who has worked with Dave Crosby and Leon Russell, he and Shalom Levine are the Megama Duo, performers of rock-flavored Jewish music.

WARREN ZEVON—Hard rocking singer-songwriter-guitarist.

IRV ZUCKERMAN—Leading rock promoter in St. Louis and Kansas City.

Don't Quite Make It

1. PAT BENATAR—Benatar is the name of a prominent Sephardic family, noted for kabalists and Talmudists, but Pat isn't Jewish. In fact, Benatar isn't her real name—it's Andrejewski. She is of Polish descent.

2. ALAN FREED—First of the great rock 'n roll disc jockeys. His father was Jewish, but he was a Methodist, as was his mother.

3. OLIVIA NEWTON-JOHN—The granddaughter of Nobel laureate Jewish physicist Max Born, she is not a Jew herself.

4. DIANA ROSS—She isn't, but her ex-husband was, and so are her children, who converted and attend Jewish schools.

5. CARLY SIMON—Singer, songwriter, married to James Taylor. Her hits include "You're So Vain." She says she's one-quarter Jewish.

6. RINGO STARR—Often called the "Jewish Beatle," he isn't.

7. CAT STEVENS—It used to be rumored that his real name is Steven Katz. It's not. Stevens is of Greek extraction. He recently became a Moslem and changed his name to Yusef Islam.

8. SLY STONE—Don't let that Star of David medallion he wears fool you.

PART TWO
REFERENCES TO JEWS OR JEWISH THEMES
IN ROCK AND COUNTRY MUSIC

"CLAMPDOWN"—A cut from Clash's 1979 album *London Calling*. It includes a line that asks, "Is this man a Jew?"

"EGYPT, ISRAEL, AMERICA"—A Seals and Crofts song on the unlikely subject of the Mid-East peace negotiations.

"GIVE PEACE A CHANCE"—John Lennon's 1969 anthem featured the line, "Everybody's talking 'bout . . . rabbis and Popeye and bye-bye, bye-bye."

INITIAL SUCCESS—One of the heroes on this 1980 album of short-story songs by B.A. Robertson, performs at bar mitzvahs on his climb to pop stardom.

"ISRAEL"—A track from the Bee Gees' 1970 album *Odessa*, this is easily the most Zionist rock number ever recorded. Not a bad tune either.

"JEWISH"—A rock version of the Jewish song "Hineh Mah Tov," played by Spirit on their 1968 album *The Family That Plays Together.*

"JEWISH PRINCESS"—A satire from Frank Zappa's 1979 album *Sheik Yerbouti.*

JOHN WESLEY HARDING—Bob Dylan's 1968 album, rich in Jewish and Biblical motifs.* By the way, if you take the "J" and the "H" from John, the "W" from Wesley, and the "H" from Harding, what have you got?

KINKY FRIEDMAN—Virtually the entire body of this country musician's work is based on Jewish themes.

---

*I have refrained from citing rock songs based on Biblical themes, except in this case, where they are clearly an expression of the artist's Jewishness.

JEWISH TOURIST—I don't know if the members of this Tucson group are Jewish or what their music is about, but they make this list on the strength of their name alone.

"PALESTINE: YOURS OR MINE?"—A 1981 single by Alienation. Hardly the most trenchant analysis of the question.

LITTLE DREAMER—A Peter Green solo album released in 1980, containing many allusions to the artist's Jewish heritage.

"NOTHING"—In this song from the 1968 Fugs album *Virgin Fugs*, a traditional Hasidic tune and nonsensical lyrics (some of them in Yiddish) combine with humorous results.

RELEASE OF AN OATH—A 1968 album by the Electric Prunes based on the Kol Nidre, the most solemn prayer of the Jewish liturgy, inaugurating the Day of Atonement.

"BABY YOU'RE A RICH MAN"—Toward the end of this 1967 hit, the Beatles sing a line that sounds like "Baby, you're a rich fag Jew," probably a reference to their manager, Brian Epstein.

THE SEX BRISTOLS—This punk rock group, also known as the 4 Be 2's has been playing anti-Semitic songs directed against Jewish fans of the Tottenham Hotspurs soccer team. A typical lyric, "Come back, Hitler. We love you."

This may not be the first instance of anti-Semitic rock. One of the biggest hits of the twist craze of 1961 was "The Peppermint Twist," by Joey Dee and the Starlighters. This song featured a series of nonsense syllables that sounded like "hey shoo ba fa ya ma ma shoo ba" repeated a number of times throughout the song. A number of folks have told me that if you play the 45-RPM record at 33 1/3, this line comes out clearly as, "Hey, Jew boy—your mama, Jew boy." It's difficult if not impossible to believe that's intentional, though.

"SHATTERED"—This track from the 1978 Rolling Stones album

Some Girls has a line about selling shmatas on Seventh Avenue.

TWO JEWS' BLUES—A 1969 album by Barry Goldberg and Mike Bloomfield.

"THE UNIVERSAL SOLDIER"—Donovan's 1965 anti-war ditty described "the universal soldier" as having seven different religions, one of them Jewish.

WASHINGTON SQUARE—Title of the Village Stompers' 1963 hit album which features a country-western banjo pickin' version of the Jewish hymn "Adon Olam."

"WAITING FOR THE WORMS"—A cut from Pink Floyd's 1979 album *The Wall* is about a neo-fascist's vision of the future in which purification of the racial strain includes turning on the showers and firing the ovens for "coons, reds, queers, and Jews." It caused a mild uproar in Israel in 1980 when listeners misconstrued it as an advocacy of fascism and genocide by Pink Floyd.

Forty-two Jazz Jews with the Instruments for Which They are Best Known

1. BARRY ALTSCHUL—Drums
2. MIKE ALTSCHUL—Woodwinds
3. RED BALABAN—Bass
4. RUBY BRAFF—Trumpet
5. BARBARA CARROLL—Piano
6. GEORGE COHEN—Trumpet
7. AL COHN—Sax
8. ALAN EAGER—Sax
9. ZIGGY ELMAN—Trumpet
10. DAVID FRIEDMAN—Vibraphone
11. DAVE FRISHBERG—Piano
12. STAN GETZ—Sax

13. BENNY GOODMAN—Clarinet
14. DANNY GOTTFRIED*—Piano
15. STEVEN GROSSMAN—Sax
16. ROMAN HAMMER**—Sax
17. CHUCK ISRAELS—Bass
18. ARELE KAMINSKY*—Drums
19. MAX KAMINSKY—Trumpet
20. DILL KATZ—Bass
21. RICHARD KATZ—Piano
22. BROOKS KERR—Piano
23. MOE KOFFMAN—Flute
24. ROMAN KUNSMAN**—Sax, flute
25. ARNIE LAWRENCE—Sax
26. MARC LEVIN—Cornet, flute
27. ALAN LEVITT—Drums
28. HANK LEVY—Sax
29. LOU LEVY—Piano
30. DAVE LIEBMAN—Sax
31. MICKEY MARKOVITZ**—Drums
32. BUDDY MORROW—Trombone
33. HERBIE MANN—Flute
34. RED RODNEY—Trumpet
35. EDDY ROZONOV**—Bass
36. ARTIE SHAW—Clarinet
37. HARVIE SWARTZ—Bass
38. SOL YAGED—Clarinet
39. PETE YELLIN—Sax
40. DANNY ZEITLIN—Piano, synthesizer
41. BARRY ZWEIG—Guitar, violin
42. MICHAEL ZWERIN—Trumpet

---

*denotes Israelis
**denotes Soviet immigrants to Israel

8.
Business

FIVE JEWISH FIRSTS IN AMERICAN BUSINESS

1. The first millionaire in America was Harmon Hendricks, a Sephardic Jew, who also founded America's first copper rolling mill in the late 1700s.
2. The first drug store in America was opened by David de Leon in the early 1800s.
3. The first gas station in America was opened by the father-and-son team of Louis and Jacob Blaustein in Baltimore in 1910.
4. The first hot-dog stand in America was opened by Abraham and Sarah Levis in Philadelphia in 1895. It is still doing business today under the name of Old Original Levis Hot Dogs.
5. The first commercial parking lot in America was opened by Max Goldberg in Detroit in 1918.

Sources: (1) Stephen Birmingham, *The Grandees;* (2-3) Ande Manners, *Poor Cousins;* (4) Dr. Levis A. Kochin of the University of Washington, grandson of Abraham and Sarah Levis; (5) *The Jewish Digest.*

One Hundred and Six Jewish Innovators and Leaders in Business

1. CHARLES FLEISCHMANN—His exhibit at Philadelphia's 1876 Centennial Exhibition, showing how to make yeast as a by-product of distilling liquor, was a sensation which led to the success of the Fleischmann Co.
2. JOHN D. HERTZ—Founder of Chicago's Yellow Cab Co.
3. ALBERT D. LASKER—Known as "the father of modern advertising," Lasker's agency was the first to not only sell space for advertisements but actually write the ads.
4. WILLIAM ROSENTHAL—Founder of Maidenform Bra Co.
5. WILLIAM FOX—Founder of 20th-Century-Fox Film Corporation.
6. JOSEPH FELLS—Founder of Fels-Naphtha Soap Co.
7. HIRSCH MANISCHEWITZ—Founder of Manischewitz Foods.
8–10. SAM GOLDWYN, LOUIS B. MAYER, MARCUS LOEW—Founders of M-G-M motion picture studios.
11. IRVING STONE—President of American Greeting Cards.
12. ISRAEL MATZ—Founder of Ex-Lax Co.
13. ADOLPH OCHS—The publisher who made *The New York Times* one of the world's leading papers.
14. CARL LAEMMLE—Founder of Universal Pictures.
15–17. BENNETT CERF, ELMER ADLER, DONALD KLOPFER—Founders of Random House publishing company.
18. HARRY M. WARNER—Founder of Warner Brothers Motion Pictures Studios.
19. SOL LINOWITZ—Former chairman of the board of Xerox Corporation.
20–21. JOSEPH and IRA BREGSTEIN—Founders of New York's Breakstone Dairies.
22. ELI BLACK—Founder of United Brands Company, a con-

glomerate which controls Baskin-Robbins ice cream and United Fruit Company, among others.

23. BEN PAUKER—Founder of Pauker Bros. sportswear.

24. ABRAHAM LEVITT—Founder of Levitt and Sons, the building firm which built Levittown communitites in Long Island, New Jersey, and Pennsylvania.

25. DR. ARMAND HAMMER—A physician who didn't go into business until he was in his fifties, Hammer is chairman of the board of Occidental Petroleum and a leading figure in trade between the U.S. and U.S.S.R.

26. JOHN M. BRUNSWICK—Founder of Brunswick Corporation, manufacturers of bowling and billiards equipment.

27. HARRY COHN—Founder of Columbia Pictures.

28. DAVID SARNOFF—President of both RCA and NBC, in their early years.

29. BOB ARUM—The world's leading boxing promoter, he staged the Ali-Spinks bout and broke racial barriers by holding the Big John Tate-Gerrie Coetzee match in Pretoria, South Africa, before an integrated crowd. Arum is an Orthodox Jew and pre-arranges a minyan (the quorum of ten Jewish men needed to conduct public prayer services) whenever he travels outside his native New York.

30. HERBERT A. AXELROD—Millionaire tropical-fish breeder and the world's greatest expert on tropical fish.

31–32. RICHARD SIMON, M.M. SCHUSTER—Founders of Simon and Schuster Publishing Co.

33. MICHEL FRIBOURG—Owner of Continental Grain Co., the largest wheat exporter to the U.S.S.R.

34. SAMUEL BRONFMAN—Founder of Distillers Corp.-Seagram, Ltd., at one time the richest man in all of Canada.

35. IRVING SHAPIRO—Former Chairman of the Board of Directors of Du Pont.

36. ADOLPH ZUKOR—Founder of Paramount Pictures.

37. EMANUEL L. WOLF—Chairman of Allied Artists Picture Corporation.

38. BOB WOOLF—The top agent for athletes in the United States and Canada.

39. BEN FIXMAN—Founder and chairman of the board of Diversified Industries, Inc., a *Fortune*-500 conglomerate.

40–42. AVI, RALPH, AND JOE NAKASH—Israeli emigrants to the U.S. who produce the popular Jordache jeans.

43–44. PHILIP and MAX STOLLMAN—Builders of the largest apartment complex in greater Detroit.

45. ANDRE-GUSTAVE CITROEN—Founder of one of France's greatest automobile companies.

46. NORMAN LEAR—Head of Tandem Productions, top producer of TV situation comedies.

47. SIDNEY WEINBERG—Member of the board of Ford Motor Co. He laid the plans for the Ford Foundation.

48. MARCUS SAMUEL—Founder of Shell Oil Co., he was later created Viscount Bearsted.

49. AUGUST BRENTANO—Founder of the Brentano's Bookstore chains.

50. KALONYMUS ZE'EV WISSOTZKY—The most successful tea merchant in Tsarist Russia.

51–52. ABRAM N. and JACK PRITZKER—Heads of the family that possesses one of two Jewish billion-dollar fortunes in America. Holdings include Hyatt Hotels, Hammond Organs, and many others.

53. SAMUEL I. NEWHOUSE—Owner of the Newhouse chain of newspapers, magazines, TV and radio stations, and Random House.

54. MARVIN DAVIS—Owner of Davis Oil Company and Twentieth Century-Fox Motion Picture Studios. America's only Jewish billionaire in his own right.

55. WALTER HAAS, JR.—President of Levi Strauss and Company, world's largest producer of jeans. Son of former Levi Strauss president Walter Haas, Sr.

56. PETER HAAS—Chairman of the Board of Levi Strauss and Company. Brother of Walter Haas.

57–58. HENRY and LESTER CROWN—Heads of a business empire estimated to be worth over $400 million, including large holdings in Hilton Hotels, General Dynamics, the St. Louis Blues hockey team, and the New York Yankees.

59. WALTER ANNENBERG—Owner of Triangle Publications, publisher of *TV Guide*, *Seventeen*, two Philadelphia newspapers, and owner of many television and radio stations.

60. LEON HESS—Chairman of the Board of Amerada Hess Corporation, an oil and chemical company.

61. IRVING HARRIS—He made his fortune as an executive and stockhold in the Toni home-permanent company and Gillette safety razors.

62–64. HYMAN, SAMUEL, and WILLIAM BELZBERG—Their holdings in Far West Financial Corporation and First City Financial Corporation put them among Western Canada's leading bankers.

65. LOUIS ARONSON—Founder of Ronson Corporation, of cigarette-lighter fame.

66. RAYMOND EPSTEIN—Chairman of the Board of A. Epstein and Sons International, Inc., a leading construction and engineering company.

67. SIDNEY EPSTEIN—President of A. Epstein and Sons International, Inc.

68. KATHARINE GRAHAM—Chairman of the Board of the Washington Post Company.

69. SAM ISRAEL, JR.—Director of Leon Israel and Brothers coffee importers and the Times-Picayune Publishing Company, publishers of New Orleans' leading newspaper.

70. LEONARD BLOCK—Chairman of the Board of Block Drug Company, a national drugstore chain.

71. HAROLD GUINZBURG—Founder of the Literary Guild in 1925.

72. NATHAN CUMMINGS—Founder of Consolidated Foods Corporation.

73. LEONARD DAVIS—Insurance magnate, who founded the Colonial Penn Group.

74. MAX FISHER—Former Chairman of the Board of Aurora Gasoline Company and United Brands.

75. HARRY GORDON—Chairman of the Board of Gordon Jewelry Corporation, an international chain of retail jewelry stores.

76. MAURICE R. GREENBERG—President of the American International Group insurance company.

77. IRWIN JACOBS—Chairman of the Board of Jacobs Industries, an investment company with holdings in a host of enterprises, mostly in the Minneapolis area.

78. ISAAC H. KEMPNER III—One of the owners of Galveston's Imperial Sugar Company and Chairman of the Board of the Sugarland Telephone company.

79. SAMUEL J. LEFRAK—One of the leading builders in New York.

80. FRED SHOCHET—Founder of Insty-Prints, America's third largest franchise printing operation.

81. MILTON PETRIE—Founder of Petrie Stores, women's clothiers.

82-83. LAURENCE and PRESTON TISCH—Owners of Loew's

Theaters and Tisch Hotels. Large holdings in Lorillard Tobacco Company.

84. NORTON SIMON—Founder of Norton Simon Inc., producers of soft drinks and other foods.

85. JULES STEIN—Founder of MCA Inc., one of America's largest producers of records and motion pictures.

86. LEAH GOTTLEIB—Founder of Gottex Industries, world's most prestigious producer of high-fashion swimwear.

87. ELI TIMONER—President of Air Florida, one of the few Jews at the top echelon of the airline business.

88–89. ALBERT and PAUL REICHMANN—The builders of 20 million square feet of office space in Canada and the largest holders of office space in New York. All of their businesses are closed on the Sabbath. The Reichmann's are very likely the wealthiest Jews in the world, with estimates of their wealth running into multiple billions.

90. JOSEPH MEYERHOFF—Founder of Monumental Properties, Inc. (formerly Joseph Meyerhoff Corporation), one of Baltimore's largest investment companies.

91. VICTOR POSNER—Miami multimillionaire with holdings in Sharon Steel, NVF Industries, National Propane Corporation, and many more. A founder of Miami's Mt. Sinai Hospital.

92. CARROLL ROSENBLOOM—Known mainly as the owner of the Los Angeles Rams and the Baltimore Colts, Rosenbloom made his fortune, estimated in excess of $75 million, in the clothing industry.

93–94. MARK and HART HASTEN—Indianapolis banking, building, and geriatrics magnates. Among Americans whose yearly incomes regularly exceed $500,000, the Hasten brothers are reputed to contribute the largest percentage of their earnings to charitable fields, largely to Jewish religious institutions.

95. MERRILL LEE BANK—Chairman of the Board of Maryland Cup Corporation.

96. HENRY SHAPIRO—President of Maryland Cup Corporation.

97. CHARLES E. SMITH—Founder of Charles E. Smith Company, one of Washington's biggest real estate companies.

98. LEW WASSERMAN—Chairman of the Board of MCA, Inc.

99. MELVIN SIMON—America's second largest builder of shopping centers.

100. HERBERT S. EPSTEIN—President of Rath Packing Company, America's largest employee-owned company.

101. ROBERT HAAG—One of the founders of Alberto-Culver Company.

102. VIDAL SASSOON—Head of a $60-million empire of health and beauty products.

103–104. YAIR and HOWARD LEVY—Israeli-born brothers who founded Ferrari Jeans.

105–106. HARRY SCHERMAN and MAX SACKHEIM—Founders of the Book-of-the-Month Club in 1926.

TWENTY-FIVE DEPARTMENT STORES AND DEPARTMENT STORE CHAINS FOUNDED OR OWNED BY JEWS

1. MACY'S-New York
2. GIMBEL'S—New York
3. BLOOMINGDALE'S—New York
4. RICH'S—Atlanta

5. NIEMANN-MARCUS—Texas
6. KAUFMANN'S—Pennsylvania
7. SEARS AND ROEBUCK—U.S.
8. E.J. KORVETTE'S—U.S.

No, it does not stand for "Eight Jewish Korean Veterans." According to Arthur Ephron (known to New Yorkers as Uncle Art of Redi-Cut Carpets), quoted in cousin Nora Ephron's *Scribble Scribble*, "The 'E' is for Eugene Ferkauf, the 'J' is for Joe Zwillenberg, and Korvette is the name of a sub chaser in WW II."

9. MYER EMPORIUM—Melbourne, Australia
10. MARSHALL'S—Adelaide, Australia
11. FILENE'S—Boston
12. B. ALTMAN—New York
13. STERN'S—New York
14. SAKS—New York
15. MARKS AND SPENCER—Great Britain
16. WOOLWORTH'S—South Africa
17. OHRBACH'S—New York
18. S. KLEIN'S—New York
19. GREAT UNIVERSAL STORES—Great Britain
20. O. K. BAZAARS—South Africa
21. LOEHMANN'S—New York
22. LEWIS'—Great Britain
23. FRANKLIN SIMON—New York
24. JOHN JACK'S—Johannesburg and Pretoria, South Africa
25. ABRAHAM AND STRAUS—New York

To find even more, see Robert Hendrickson's book *The Grand Emporiums*.

Six Cosmetics Companies Founded by Jews

1. REVLON
2. MAX FACTOR
3. HELENA RUBINSTEIN
4. FABERGÉ
5. ESTÉE LAUDER
6. ADRIEN ARPEL

9.
Israel

THE MOST AND LEAST DESIRED PROFESSIONS IN ISRAEL

In September 1974, 1,200 Israeli parents were polled as to the three professions they would most want and least want their children to enter. The results:

MOST DESIRED
1. doctor
2. scientist
3. teacher
4. lawyer
5. professor
6. journalist
7. industrialist
8. building contractor
9. military officer
10. El Al pilot

LEAST DESIRED
1. political party official
2. member of Knesset
3. bus driver
4. kibbutz member
5. government clerk

A TABLE OF ISRAELI FIRSTS

JULY 1948—The Israeli Air Force makes its first raid on Cairo.

JANUARY 1949—Israel's first wheat imports from Russia.

MARCH 1949—Inauguration of phone service to the United States and Canada.

JULY 1949—Israel's first traffic light goes on in Haifa.

JULY 1949—El Al's first New York-Tel Aviv flight.

SEPTEMBER 1949—Israel prints its first telephone directory.

MARCH 1950—Israel radio begins English language shortwave broadcasts. President Chaim Weizmann speaks on the first program.

NOVEMBER 1951—The beginning of telephone service to Iceland.

MAY 1952—The first graduating class from Hebrew University Medical School.

JUNE 1953—The Israeli Air Force gets its first jets, British-made Meteors.

JUNE 1953—The first exports of onions and garlic from Israel to Europe.

AUGUST 1953—The first cargo of goods coming as restitution from West Germany arrives. A threatened Arab economic boycott of West Germany never materializes.

AUGUST 1954—Jerusalem's first traffic light is put in operation.

FEBRUARY 1956—The first tourist from Russia arrives in Israel.

AUGUST 1957—Gov. Albert "Happy" Chandler of Kentucky makes Prime Minister Ben Gurion Israel's first Kentucky colonel, while visiting Israel.

JANUARY 1958—The first foreign embassy in Jerusalem is opened by the Netherlands.

SEPTEMBER 1958—Israel's first supermarket opens in Tel Aviv.

APRIL 1959—Israel's first large department store, five stories high, opens in Tel Aviv.

JULY 1959—Israel's first gnu is born in the Tel Aviv zoo.

OCTOBER 1959—The first (and, as of 1981, only) subway in Israel begins operating in Haifa.

JANUARY 1960—Congressman Seymour Halpern becomes the first U. S. Congressman to spend his honeymoon in Israel.

APRIL 1960—Israel's first golf course opens in Caesarea.

APRIL 1962—The first branch office of an Israeli bank opens in New York.

MARCH 1963—El Al serves bagel-and-lox breakfasts on its flights.

APRIL 1966—Israel begins television broadcasts.

SEPTEMBER 1967—West Bank Arabs make their first appearance on teams in the Israeli Soccer League.

APRIL 1968—Coca-Cola appears for the first time in Israel stores.

JULY 1968—Israel's merchant marine begins broadcasting messages in Hebrew Morse code.

OCTOBER 1968—The first restaurant owned jointly by Jews and Arabs opens in Jerusalem.

AUGUST 1970—Mordechai Spigler becomes the first Israeli soccer player to sign with an English team.

AUGUST 1970—The first building with escalators is built in Jerusalem.

AUGUST 1972—The first tire exports to the United States begin.

SEPTEMBER 1972—A Druse becomes the first non-Jew to attain the rank of lieutenant colonel in the Israeli army.

MAY 1973—The first known case of a father and son undergoing circumcision together at the hands of a father-and-son team of mohalim (ritual circumcisers). The subjects were recent immigrants from the Soviet Union.

MAY 1973—For the first time a Red Chinese diplomat participates at an Israeli diplomatic function. The Chinese ambassador to Greece attended a reception at the Israeli embassy in Athens honoring Israel's 25th anniversary. He

later claimed it was all a mistake and that he thought he was
at the Kuwaiti embassy. Kuwait had no embassy in Greece
at the time.

JULY 1973—The first tulip exports from Israel to Holland begin.

JULY 1975—Maha Suleiman becomes Israel's first Arab police-
woman.

NOVEMBER 1975—The first Arabic phone book is published in
Israel.

OCTOBER 1976—Jerusalem gets its first woman bus driver.

OCTOBER 1978—Direct mail service between Israel and Egypt is
inaugurated.

SEVENTEEN JEWISH ANTI-ZIONISTS
AND ONE PALESTINIAN ZIONIST

1. HYMAN LUMAR—Editor of the U.S. Communist Party publication *Jewish Affairs.*
2. ELMER BERGER—Founder of the American Council for
   Judaism, an organization of Reform Jews opposed to the
   Reform movement's rejection of its earlier anti-Zionist position in 1937. Berger is currently affiliated with a group called
   Jewish Alternatives to Zionism and lectures on college
   campuses under the sponsorship of the General Union of
   Palestinian Students.
3. RABBI JOEL TEITELBAUM—Leader of the anti-Zionist Satmar
   Hasidic sect. He rejected Zionism because of the tendency
   of some Jews to view its espousal as a substitute for adherence to the laws of the Jewish religion. When approached
   by members of the American Council for Judaism with a
   proposal for joint anti-Zionist activity, Rabbi Teitelbaum
   rejected the offer. "For us the State of Israel is not enough,"
   he explained. "For you it is too much." Rabbi Teitelbaum
   died in 1979 at the age of 91.

4. RUTH BLAU—Born Madeleine Ferraille, she worked with the French resistance during World War II and subsequently converted from Catholicism to Orthodox Judaism. She married Rabbi Amram Blau, head of Jerusalem's anti-Zionist *Neturei Karta* (Guardians of the City) group. Since her husband's death, Mrs. Blau has been an outspoken supporter of the P.L.O. and Ayatollah Khomeini.

5. MEIR WILNER—Head of Israel's Communist party, staunch supporters of Moscow's line.

6-7. LEAH TZEMEL and FELICIA LANGER—Supporters of Israel's Communist party, who often serve as lawyers for Palestinian terrorists.

8-9. RAMI LIVNE and MALI LERMAN—Members of Kibbutz Kfar Shmuel, who were jailed in 1974 for passing security secrets to Syria. Both are anti-Zionist leftists. Livne is the son of Communist Knesset member Avram Levenbron.

10. NOAM CHOMSKY—Noted American linguist who has come out in favor of the P.L.O. after involvement in the socialist Hashomer Hatzair Zionist organization in his youth.

11. MATYAS RAKOSI—Hungary's Communist dictator from 1949 to 1956. He conducted a number of trials against Zionists.

12. SIR EDWARD MONTAGU—British Secretary of State for India in 1917. He had Arthur Balfour water down the language of the Balfour Declaration because of his fear of anti-Semitic reaction to it, thereby creating a problem that was to plague Zionists for decades.

13. ROBERT STEINHORN—A leader of the Progressive Labor Party, successor to the Students for a Democratic Society (S.D.S.), Steinhorn has written articles attacking Israel in the press of the New Left.

14. MOSHE MENUHIN—German journalist and father of violinist

Yehudi Menuhin. He once denounced a Munich neo-Nazi magazine for not being sufficiently hostile to Israel. Menuhim *fils* has dissociated himself from his father's views.

15. LESSING ROSENWALD—Former chairman of the board of Sears Roebuck and Company and chairman of the American Council for Judaism. When visiting Prime Minister Ben-Gurion in Israel in 1957, Rosenwald described himself as anti-Zionist but not anti-Israel; that is, he objected to the idea of Israel being a home for all Jews.

16. RITA FREED—Former chairperson of the Committee to Support Middle East Liberation, a pro-Arab, Trotskyite group.

17. NORMAN TEMPLE—Chairman of the British Anti-Zionist Organization. This organization has been ousted from the National Union of Students for alleged anti-Semitism. What prompted the ouster was BAZO's reported claim that Anne Frank never existed and that her story was no more than a Zionist hoax.

18. YASSER JABRIN-LACHMOUZ—The subject of an article in the July 4, 1980, issue of the Jerusalem weekly *Kan Yerushalayim* (Here's Jerusalem), Jabrin-Lachmouz is a 25-year-old Palestinian from the Hebron area who became convinced that Israel rightfully belongs to the Jews when, at the age of eighteen, he first read the Bible. Jabrin-Lachmouz now leads a lonely life in Jerusalem, ostracized by Arabs and held in suspicion by Jews. His recent application for Israeli citizenship was rejected.

THREE GENTILE ZIONISTS WHO RECANTED

1. JOSEPH STALIN—According to records of the Yalta Conference, released on March 17, 1955, Stalin referred to himself

as a Zionist. The record of the February 10, 1945, session reads, "The President (Roosevelt) said he was a Zionist and asked if Marshal Stalin was one. Marshal Stalin said he was one in principle but he recognized the difficulty."

It seems that the difficulty got the best of Stalin. He subsequently killed and imprisoned large numbers of Jews on the charge of "Zionism" in the late 1940s and early 50s and displayed hostility toward Israel, after his early support of the fledgling state.

2. DR. DIANE CAMPBELL-LEFEBVRE—This British physician was among those apprehended while on a mission to bomb the Israeli embassy in Paris in April 1973. She was once an ardent Zionist, engaged to a Jew, and considered converting to Judaism, but her sympathies shifted when her engagement broke up.

3. SPIRO AGNEW—A strong supporter of Israel during his days as a successful politician, Agnew was the guest speaker at the 1972 banquet of the Religious Zionists of America. By 1976, the disgraced former Vice President was whistling a different tune when he attacked Israeli "imperialism and aggression" and warned of Zionist influences in the United States on NBC-TV's *Today Show.*

THREE LIBEL RULINGS BY ISRAELI COURTS

1. In a 1977 ruling, a Tel Aviv court ruled that calling a Jew an "anti-Zionist" without cause was a libelous insult.

2. In 1979, a Jerusalem court ruled that calling someone a "yekke" (slang for German Jew) was not a libelous insult.

3. In 1973, an Ashkelon court fined a man for calling Ashkelon's mayor an idiot. The court made it clear that the fine was for

insulting the mayor while he was working in his official capacity. It is permitted to call a mayor an idiot after office hours.

MENACHEM BEGIN'S LIST OF MOST INSPIRING NATIONALISTS

1. THEODORE HERZL
2. VLADIMIR JABOTINSKY—Founder of Revisionist Zionism
3. GUISEPPE GARIBALDI—Nineteenth-century Italian revolutionary

RELIGIOUS BREAKDOWN OF JERUSALEM'S POPULATION

Year	Jewish	Moslem	Christian	Total
1844	7,120	5,000	3,390	15,510
1876	12,000	7,560	5,470	25,030
1896	28,112	8,560	8,748	45,420
1905	40,000	7,000	13,000	60,000
1913	48,400	10,050	16,750	75,200
1922	33,971	13,413	14,699	62,083
1931	51,522	19,894	19,335	90,451
1948	100,000	40,000	25,000	165,000
1967	195,700	54,963	10,800	261,463
1973	222,100	67,000	12,000	301,100
1980	285,000	83,000	17,000	385,000

10.

The Military

ELEVEN JEWISH BUCCANEERS AND PIRATES

1. SUBATOL DEUL—He operated off South America's Pacific coast and formed an alliance with Henry Drake, son of Sir Francis Drake, called the Brotherhood of the Black Flag. Deul maintained that it was his father who introduced the potato to Europe, not Sir Francis. Henry Drake never disputed this claim.

2. SINAN PASHA—A sixteenth-century Jewish pirate feared throughout Europe and Asia. Sinan often worked in conjunction with Khair-ed-Din-Barbarossa and the Turks against Christian forces and scored formidable victories against the Knights of St. John of Malta. He was named Admiral-General of the Turkish navy in 1550, three years before his death.

3. DON SHMUEL PALACHE—This seventeenth-century pirate allied himself with the Moroccans and the Dutch and was the scourge of Portuguese and Spanish shipping. Palache was also a rabbi and founded Amsterdam's first synagogue.

4–6. SAMPSON SIMON, HAYMAN LEVY, JUDAH HAY—Priva-

teers who raided French shipping during the French and
Indian War.

7-10. MOSES HAYS, ISAAC MOSES, BENJAMIN SEIXAS, AARON
LOPEZ—Privateers who raided British shipping during the
American War of Independence.

11. JEAN LAFITTE—The pirate and adventurer who collaborated with Andrew Jackson to defeat the British at New
Orleans. In his diary he revealed that his maternal grand-
parents (and thus, his mother and he himself) were Jewish
and suffered at the hands of the Spanish Inquisition.

Sources: (1) *Jerusalem Post,* July 1, 1979; (2–3) *Jerusalem Post,*
June 15, 1979; (4–10) Stanley Feldstein, *The Land That I
Show You;* (11) *Jewish Digest,* Vol. I, no. 9.

Numbers of Enemy Aircraft Destroyed by the Israeli Air Force

War of Independence 21
Sinai Campaign 7
Six Day War 451
War of Attrition 116
Yom Kippur War . . . . 425 (approximate)
Between wars 127

Numbers of Jewish Dead in Action who Served in the Armed Forces of Several Allied Countries During World War II*

1. United States . . . . . . 11,000 (approximate)
2. Great Britain 1,279

3. Canada 776
4. South Africa 283
5. Australia 117
6. Palestine's Jewish Brigade 500
                              (approximate)
7. Poland 32,216

*Only these figures are available. Note that substantial numbers of Jews died in the armed forces of France, other European and western hemisphere nations, and especially the Soviet Union.

EIGHT EUROPEAN JEWISH MILITARY HEROES

1. COLONEL MORDECHAI FRIZIS—Known simply as "the Jewish Colonel," Frizis was one of the most talented officers of the Greek Army. He was killed in battle in 1940 during the Italian invasion. The Greek town of Bessanchi was renamed Frizisville in his memory.

2. LT. GEN. MATVEI VAINRUB—Mentioned frequently by Marshal Zhukov in his account of the Battle of Stalingrad as being a crucial figure in the defense of that city, he was one of the few commanders surviving that battle whose military career did not advance. Vainrub was named a Hero of the Soviet Union.

3. LEV DOVATOR—The only Jewish commander of the notoriously anti-Semitic Cossacks, General Dovator died in the Battle of Moscow in 1941. The Soviet government honored him in 1942 by printing a postage stamp bearing his likeness.

4. ILYA KATUNIN—A flight commander, he was posthumously named a Hero of the Soviet Union after his kamikaze-like attack on a German warship in World War II.

5. ABRAHAM LEVY—He was one of the first Jews to be

appointed a brigadier general in the French Army. Levy could have advanced his career by converting to Christianity but refused to do so.

6. GEN. SIR JOHN MONASH—Commander of the Australian troops in World War I, Monash is often considered the ablest British Empire general of that war.

7. GEN. JACOB SHMUSHKEVITCH—Commander-in-chief of the Soviet Air Force at the onset of World War II, Shmushkevitch died when the fighter he was piloting was shot down by the Germans.

8. ISRAEL FISANOVICH—Considered one of the most skilled submarine commanders in the Soviet navy, he was awarded the Navy Cross by the U.S. Navy. Fisanovich died when his submarine was sunk in 1943.

FIVE JEWS WHO PARTICIPATED IN THE BOMBING OF HIROSHIMA AND NAGASAKI

The Jewish contribution to the invention of the atom bomb has been written about sufficiently to make a list of those names superfluous. What isn't so well known is the Jewish role in the dropping of the bomb.

1. LT. JACOB BESSER—He was on the plane that dropped the bomb on Nagasaki and also took part in the Hiroshima mission.

2. SGT. ABE SPITZER—Radio operator for one of the observation planes in the Hiroshima mission and for the plane that dropped the bomb on Nagasaki.

3. CAPT. CHARLES LEVY—Bombardier for one of the Nagasaki observation planes.

4. LT. FREDERICK CHARNES—Navigator of a plane that photographed Nagasaki after the bombing.

5. E. KOVAC—Navigator of one of the two British planes involved in the attacks. He spent most of his time in the air reciting the Psalms.

11.
Judaica Americana

EIGHT JEWS WHO HAVE APPEARED ON AMERICAN POSTAGE STAMPS

1. RABBI ALEXANDER D. GOODE—One of the four chaplains on the U.S.S. *Dorchester* who gave his life preserver to another soldier and went down with the ship during World War II. Rabbi Goode is one of only two rabbis to appear on stamps outside of Israel, the other being Rabbi Leo Baeck on a British stamp.
2. SAMUEL GOMPERS
3. ALBERT EINSTEIN—Twice
4. GEORGE GERSHWIN
5. HAYM SOLOMON
6. FIORELLO LA GUARDIA—The New York mayor didn't consider himself a Jew but his mother was a Hungarian Jewess.
7. ADOLPH OCHS
8. ABIGAIL FRANKS
9. PHILIP BLAIBERG—The only Jew to have appeared on a stamp issued by an Arab country was Dr. Philip Blaiberg, Dr. Christian Barnard's second heart transplant patient. He and

Dr. Barnard were portrayed on a stamp issued by the Yemen Arab Republic in 1969. Dr. Barnard's first heart transplant patient, Louis Washkansky, was also Jewish.

Twenty-Two Jewish Winners of the Presidential Medal of Freedom

The Medal of Freedom, as it now exists, was established by President Kennedy in an Executive Order, on February 22, 1963. The award was first set up under President Truman in 1945 to reward meritorious, war-connected acts or services. The Kennedy Executive Order expanded the award to include those who should be honored for meritorious contribution to the national security or the national interest of the United States, world peace, or other significant public or private endeavors. Persons are selected for receipt of this medal by the President. The following Jews have won the award (date in parentheses):

Presented by President Eisenhower
1. LEWIS L. STRAUSS—Member of the Atomic Energy Comission (7/14/58)

Presented by President Johnson
2. AARON COPLAND—Composer (9/14/64)
3. DAVID DUBINSKY—Labor leader (1/20/69)
4. FELIX FRANKFURTER—U.S. Supreme Court Justice (12/6/63)
5. EDWARD H. LAND—Inventor (12/6/63)
6. HERBERT H. LEHMAN—New York Governor and U.S. Senator (1/28/64)

7. WALTER LIPPMANN—Journalist (9/14/64)
8. RUDOLF SERKIN—Pianist (12/6/63)

Presented by President Nixon
9. SAMUEL GOLDWYN—Motion picture magnate (3/27/71)
10. ARTHUR KROCK—Journalist (4/22/70)
11. DAVID LAWRENCE—Journalist (4/22/70)
12. EUGENE ORMANDY—Orchestra conductor (1/24/70)

Presented by President Ford
13. IRVING BERLIN—Composer (1/10/77)
14. ARTHUR FIEDLER—Orchestra conductor (1/10/77)
15. HENRY A. KISSINGER—Secretary of State (1/13/77)
16. ARTUR RUBINSTEIN—Pianist (4/1/76)

Presented by President Carter
17. HAROLD BROWN—Secretary of Defense (1/16/81)
18. KIRK DOUGLAS—Film star (1/16/81)
19. ARTHUR J. GOLDBERG—U.S. Supreme Court Justice, Secretary of Labor, and U.S. ambassador to U.N. (7/26/78)
20. ADM. HYMAN RICKOVER—Pioneer in the field of nuclear submarine technology (6/9/80)
21. DR. JONAS E. SALK—Discoverer of polio vaccine (7/11/77)
22. BEVERLY SILLS—Opera star (6/9/80)

FOUR JEWS PROMINENT IN THE CONFEDERATE STATES OF AMERICA

1. JUDAH P. BENJAMIN—A former U.S. Senator from Louisana, Benjamin served at various times as Attorney General, Secretary of War, and Secretary of State of the Confederacy.

2. DAVID YULEE—A former U.S. Senator from Florida (the first Jewish Senator), Yulee later sat in the Confederate Congress.
3. DAVID DE LEON—Surgeon General of the Confederacy.
4. ABRAHAM C. MYERS—Quartermaster-General of the Confederate Army.

FORTY-FIVE JEWS WHO HAVE HELD MAJOR AMERICAN DIPLOMATIC POSTS

1. WALTER ANNENBERG—Ambassador to Great Britain (1969–1974)
2. MORTON ABRAMOWITZ—Ambassador to Thailand (1978–1981)
3. HERMAN BARUCH—Minister to the Netherlands (1944), Minister to Portugal (1945)
4. AUGUST BELMONT—Minister to The Netherlands (1854)
5. HERMAN BERNSTEIN—Minister to Albania (1929–1933)
6. ARTHUR BURNS—Ambassador to West Germany (1981–   )
7. IRVING GOTTLIEB CHESLAW—Ambassador to Trinidad and Tobago (1979–1981)
8. THEODORE E. CUMMINGS—Ambassador to Austria (1981–1982)
9. ABRAM L. ELKUS—Ambassador to Turkey (1916–1919)
10. LEWIS EINSTEIN—Minister to Costa Rica (1911–1913), Minister to Czechoslovakia (1921–1930)
11. RUTH FARKAS—Ambassador to Luxembourg (1973–1976)
12. GEORGE FELDMAN—Ambassador to Malta (1965–1966), Ambassador to Luxembourg (1967–1969)
13. HARVY FELDMAN—Ambassador to Papua New Guinea and Solomon Islands (1979–1981)
14. MAXWELL GLUCK—Minister to Ceylon (1957–1959)

15. ARTHUR GOLDBERG—Ambassador to the United Nations (1965–1968)
16. HARRY F. GUGGENHEIM—Ambassador to Cuba (1929–1933)
17. M. ROBERT GUGGENHEIM—Ambassador to Portugal (1953–1954)
18. SOLOMON HIRSCH—Minister to Turkey (1889–1892)
19. DAVID S. KAUFMAN—Minister to Bolivia (1928–1930), Minister to Thailand (1930–1933)
20. JOSEPH F. KORNFELD—Minister to Iran (1921–1924)
21. LEO A. LERNER—Ambassador to Sweden (1977–1980)
22. SOL LINOWITZ—Special envoy to the Mid-East Peace Negotiations (1979–1980)
23. JOHN L. LOEB—Ambassador to Denmark (1981–   )
24. FREDERICK MANN—Ambassador to Barbados (1966–1969)
25. WARREN MANSHEL—Ambassador to Denmark (1978–1981)
26. HENRY MORGANTHAU, SR.—Ambassador to Turkey (1913–1916)
27. IRA NELSON MORRIS—Minister to Sweden (1914–1923)
28. ROBERT NEUMANN*—Ambassador to Afghanistan (1966–1973), Ambassador to Morocco (1973–1976), Ambassador to Saudi Arabia (1981)
29. MARCUS OTTERBOURG—Minister to Mexico (1867)
30. BENJAMIN F. PEIXOTTO—Consul General to Rumania (1870–1876)
31. MAXWELL RAAB—Ambassador to Italy (1981–   )
32. ABRAM C. RATCHESKY—Minister to Czechoslovakia (1930–1932)
33. WILLIAM RIVKIN—Ambassador to Luxembourg (1962–1965), Ambassador to Senegal and The Gambia (1966–1967)

*See converts to Christianity, page 33 ff.

34. LEO R. SACK—Minister to Costa Rica (1933–1937)
35. WILLIAM B. SCHWARTZ—Ambassador to the Bahamas (1977–1981)
36. LAURENCE HIRSCH SILBERMAN—Ambassador to Yugoslavia (1975–1976)
37. LAWRENCE A. STEINHARDT—Minister to Sweden (1933–1937), Ambassador to Peru (1937, 1939), Ambassador to Russia (1939–1942), Ambassador to Turkey (1942–1945), Ambassador to Czechoslovakia (1945–1948), Ambassador to Canada (1959–1960)
38. JESSE ISIDOR STRAUS—Ambassador to France (1933–1936)
39. OSCAR S. STRAUS—Ambassador to Turkey (1887–1890, 1897–1900, 1909–1910)
40. ROBERT STRAUSS—Special envoy to the Mid-East Peace Negotiations (1978–1979)
41. MARVIN L. WARNER—Ambassador to Switzerland (1977–1979)
42. SEYMOUR WEISS—Ambassador to The Bahamas (1974–1976)
43. MARVIN WEISSMAN—Ambassador to Costa Rica (1977–1980), Ambassador to Bolivia (1980)
44. MILTON WOLF—Ambassador to Austria (1977–1980)
45. JAMES D. ZELLERBACH—Ambassador to Italy (1956–1958)

JEWISH GOVERNORS
Governors of States

1. Moses Alexander (D), Idaho 1915-1923
2. Simon Bamberger (D), Utah 1917-1921
3. Arthur Seligman (D), New Mexico 1931-1933
4. Julius Meier (R), Oregon 1931-1934
5. Henry Horner (D), Illinois 1933-1940
6. Herbert Lehman (D), New York 1933-1942

7. Abraham Ribicoff (D), Connecticut 1955-1961
8. Samuel Shapiro (D), Illinois 1968
9. Frank Licht (D), Rhode Island 1969-1972
10. Marvin Mandel (D), Maryland 1969–1977
11. Milton J. Shapp (D), Pennsylvania 1971–1979

Governors of Territories

12. Edward Solomon (R), Washington 1872-1874
13. Ernest Gruening (D), Alaska 1939-1953
14. Morris de Castro (D), Virgin Islands 1950-1954
15. Ralph Paiewonsky (D), Virgin Islands 1961-1967

THIRTEEN JEWS WHO HAVE SERVED AS U.S. CABINET SECRETARIES

1. OSCAR STRAUS—Secretary of Commerce and Labor under Theodore Roosevelt.
2. HENRY MORGENTHAU, JR.—Secretary of the Treasury under Franklin Delano Roosevelt and Harry S. Truman
3. ABRAHAM RIBICOFF—Secretary of Health, Education and Welfare under John F. Kennedy
4. ARTHUR GOLDBERG—Secretary of Labor under John F. Kennedy
5. WILBUR COHEN—Secretary of Health, Education and Welfare under Lyndon B. Johnson
6. HENRY A. KISSINGER—Secretary of State under Richard Nixon and Gerald Ford
7. EDWARD LEVI—Attorney General under Gerald Ford
8. JAMES SCHLESINGER*—Secretary of Defense under Gerald Ford, Secretary of Energy under James Earl Carter

*See converts to Christianity, page 33 ff.

9. HAROLD BROWN—Secretary of Defense under James Earl Carter
10. MICHAEL BLUMENTHAL*—Secretary of the Treasury under James Earl Carter
11. NEIL GOLDSCHMIDT—Secretary of Transportation under James Earl Carter
12. PHILIP KLUTZNICK—Secretary of Commerce under James Earl Carter
13. ALEXANDER HAMILTON—First Secretary of the Treasury of the United States. Although he was certainly not a practicing Jew, the facts seem to indicate that Hamilton's mother was Jewish. While there is some doubt as to who his father was, Hamilton was unquestionably the son of Rachel Fawcett Levine, wife of John Michael Levine, a Danish Jew living in the West Indies. Though she was not born Jewish, it is reasonable to assume that Levine would have had his sixteen-year-old bride convert to his religion, especially as he took her to his native Copenhagen to show her off in 1752, a time when a Jew taking a Gentile wife would have been considered scandalous. Hamilton's biographers say that he knew some Hebrew, having been taught in his youth by a Jewish schoolmistress.

Lawrence Silberman was acting Attorney General for four days in 1974 between the resignation of William Saxbe and the swearing in of Edward Levi.

Sen. Isidor Raynor of Maryland, a Jew, was about to be named to a cabinet post by Pres. Woodrow Wilson when Raynor died, in 1912. William Jennings Bryan had suggested he be nominated for vice president at the Democratic Convention that year. Wilson then wanted to name Louis Brandeis to a cabinet position but backed down when faced with stiff opposition within his own party. He named Brandeis to the Supreme Court in 1916.

Dwight D. Eisenhower nominated Lewis L. Strauss as his Secretary of Commerce in 1958 but his nomination was not confirmed by the Senate. Eisenhower's Secretary of the Treasury, Douglas Dillon, had a Jewish grandfather, Sam Lupowski.

Theodore Sorenson, nominated to head the CIA by Jimmy Carter (but not confirmed), is the son of Russian Jewish immigrant Annis Chaikin but considers himself a Christian.

JEWS IN THE 98TH CONGRESS

Senate

1. Rudy Boschwitz (R)—Minnesota
2. Jacob "Chick" Hecht (R)—Nevada
3. Frank Lautenberg (D)—New Jersey
4. Carl Levin (D)—Michigan
5. Howard Metzenbaum (D)—Ohio
6. Warren Rudman (R)—New Hampshire
7. Arlen Specter (R)—Pennsylvania
8. Edward Zorinsky (D)—Nebraska

House of Representatives

1. Anthony Beilenson (D)—California
2. Howard Berman (D)—California
3. Barbara Boxer (D)—California
4. Ben Edreich (D)—Alabama
5. Bobbi Fiedler (R)—California
6. Barney Frank (D)—Massachusetts
7. Martin Frost (D)—Texas
8. Sam Gejdenson (D)—Connecticut
9. Benjamin Gilman (R)—New York

10. Dan Glickman (D)—Kansas
11. Willis Gradison, Jr. (R)—Ohio
12. Bill Green (R)—New York
13. Ken Kramer (R)—Colorado
14. Tom Lantos (D)—California
15. William Lehman (D)—Florida
16. Sander Levin (D)—Michigan
17. Mel Levine (D)—California
18. Elliot Levitas (D)—Georgia
19. Richard Ottinger (D)—New York
20. Frederick Richmond (D)—New York
21. Benjamin Rosenthal (D)—New York
22. James Scheuer (D)—New York
23. Charles Schumer (D)—New York
24. Bob Shamansky (D)—Ohio
25. Norman Sisisky (D)—Virginia
26. Larry Smith (D)—Florida
27. Stephen Solarz (D)—New York
28. Gladys Spellman (D)—Maryland
29. Henry Waxman (D)—California
30. Theodore Weiss (D)—New York
31. Howard Wolpe (D)—Michigan
32. Sidney Yates (D)—Illinois

SENATOR CARL LEVIN'S LIST OF OUTSTANDING JEWISH-AMERICAN PUBLIC SERVANTS

Bernard Baruch
Judah Benjamin
Louis Brandeis
Samuel Gompers
Jacob Javits
Herbert Lehman

Golda Meir (yes, an American, too)
Haym Solomon

As the Senator says, "The interesting thing about writing lists is not how many names you can add on, but how few you can put down and still provide a broad range of differences."

FOUR JEWS IN THE REAGAN ADMINISTRATION

1. PAUL WOLFOWITZ—Director of the State Department's policy planning staff
2. ELLIOT ABRAMS—Assistant Secretary of State for international organizational affairs
3. RICHARD PERLE—Assistant Secretary of Defense for international security affairs
4. JACOB STEIN—White House liaison to the Jewish community

Murray Weidenbaum, who was Chairman of the Council of Economic Advisors, resigned in 1982.

U. S. Secretary of State Caspar Willard Weinberger is a practicing Episcopalian, but his paternal grandfather was a Jew from Bohemia, which explains his Jewish-sounding last name.

SEVEN JEWISH NEO-CONSERVATIVES

The neo-conservative movement in the United States came about largely as a reaction of segments of American intelligentsia to America's weak foreign policy since its defeat in the Vietnam War. Prominent at its forefront are a large number of Jewish intellectuals and academicians. Testimony to the neo-conservative movement's inroads among America's traditionally liberal Jewish population is the fact that in the 1980 elections, Jimmy Carter received only 45 percent of the Jewish vote, less than any Democratic candidate since before the days of Franklin Delano Roosevelt.

1. NORMAN PODHORETZ—Editor of *Commentary,* principal organ of the neo-conservatives.
2. MILTON HIMMELFARB—A frequent contributor to *Commentary* and a member of its editorial board.
3. SEYMOUR MARTIN LIPSET—A professor of sociology at Stanford whose political views have shifted to the right in the past decade. He is a foreign policy adviser to Sen. Daniel Patrick Moynihan, as is . . .
4. IRVING KRISTOL—Editor of *Public Interest Magazine* and professor of social thought at N.Y.U. He is the author of *Life in America* and numerous other books.
5. CARL GERSHMAN—Executive Director of Social Democrats USA and a member of the Democratic Party, he nonetheless actively supported Republican candidates in the last elections. Gershman is chief aide to U.N. Ambassador Jeanne Kirkpatrick.
6. MILTON FRIEDMAN—Nobel Prize-winning economist and best-selling author. His free-market economic theories are one of the bases of neo-conservative politics.
7. ELLIOT ABRAMS—Assistant Secretary of State for international organizational affairs, former chief of staff to Sen. Daniel Moynihan, and Norman Podhoretz's son-in-law.

Thirty-Two Jews on the Faculty of Harvard

ADAM ULAM—Professor of government
MARTIN S. FELDSTEIN—Professor of economics
MICHAEL WALZER—Professor of government
BENJAMIN SCHWARTZ—Professor of history and social science

HERBERT C. KELMAN—Richard Clarke Cabot Professor of Social Ethics

DANIEL BELL—Professor of sociology

MARTIN BLOOMFIELD—Arthur Kingsley Porter Professor of English

ISADORE TWERSKY—Director of the Center for Jewish Studies

ISRAEL SCHEFFLER—Professor of education and philosophy

CHARLES BERLIN—Lee M. Friedman Bibliographer in Judaica

ALAN DERSHOWITZ—Professor of law

RICHARD PIPES—Frank Baird, Jr., professor of history

DAVID LANDES—Professor of history

JUDITH KATES—Associate professor of English and comparative literature

NATHAN GLAZER—Professor of education and social structure

BARRY MAZUR—Professor of mathematics

DAVID KASHDAN—Professor of mathematics

STEVEN J. GOLD—Professor of geology

MARTIN WHITE—Professor of philosophy

ALBERT HIRSCHMAN—Professor of economics

I. BERNARD COHEN—Professor of history of science

STANLEY HOFFMAN—Professor of political science

GERALD COPLAN—Professor of psychiatry

NATHAN KEYFITZ—Professor of sociology

MILTON ALPER—Associate professor of anesthesiology at Harvard Medical School

HENRY ROSOVSKY—Dean of the Faculty of Arts and Sciences

STANLEY L. CAVELL—Walter M. Cabot Professor of Aesthetics and General Theory of Value

HERBERT NOZICK—Professor of philosophy

MILTON KATZ—Director of international legal studies

LOUIS L. JAFFE—Byrne Professor of Administrative Law

PAUL FREUND—Professor of law

JEROME COHEN—Professor of law

TWENTY-FOUR ACCOMPLISHED JEWISH GRADUATES OF CITY COLLEGE OF NEW YORK

Offering free tuition to New York residents, C.C.N.Y. was the first step on the road to success for many of the children of the Jewish immigrants who came to New York in the late nineteenth and early twentieth centuries. Here's a list of some of its most prominent Jewish graduates.

1. BERNARD BARUCH—Presidential adviser
2. ED KOCH—Mayor of New York
3. JONAS SALK—Discoverer of polio vaccine
4. MAX GARRET—University of Illinois fencing coach
5. ARTHUR KORNBERG—Winner of the 1959 Nobel Prize for Medicine, for the discovery of DNA
6. NAT FLEISCHER—Boxing expert, founder of *Ring* magazine
7. FELIX FRANKFURTER—U.S. Supreme Court Justice
8. NAT HOLMAN—Coach of CCNY and played on the Original Celtics
9. MORRIS RAPHAEL COHEN—Noted philosopher
10. PAUL JACOBS—Leftist leader, editor of *Ramparts* magazine
11. ADOLPHUS SIMEON SOLOMONS—Nineteenth-century politician, one of the founders of the American Red Cross
12. DAVID STEINMAN—Engineer who designed the Mackinac Bridge
13. ABE BEAME—Mayor of New York
14. PAUL WEISS—Prominent philosopher
15. ABRAHAM MICHAEL ROSENTHAL—Editor of *The New York Times*
16. LEONARD FARBSTEIN—Congressman
17. MILTON HIMMELFARB—Magazine editor, research director
18. IRVING KRISTOL—Educator
19. HOWARD SQUADRON—President of the American Jewish

Congress and chairman of the Conference of Presidents of Major American Jewish Organizations

20. DANIEL BELL—Sociologist
21. PADDY CHAYEFSKY—Playwright
22. BERNIE WEST—TV producer
23. DR. MILTON HELPERN—Chief medical examiner of the city of New York
24. DR. ALBERT ELLIS—Prominent psychologist

ELEVEN JEWS WHO GREW UP IN BROWNSVILLE

The greatest concentration of Jews in turn-of-the-century New York was, of course, on Manhattan's Lower East Side. The second largest New York Jewish community sprang up in the Brownsville area of Brooklyn. Some of the prominent Jews it spawned:

1. DANNY KAYE—Actor
2. ABE "KID TWIST" RELES—Leading figure in Murder, Incorporated
3. SOL HUROK—Impresario
4. DR. ARTHUR KORNBERG—Nobel Prize winner
5. ALFRED KAZIN—Author, critic
6. COL. DAVID "MICKEY" MARCUS—Hero of Israel's War of Independence
7. NORMAN PODHORETZ—Editor of *Commentary*
8. JOSEPH HIRSHHORN—Noted art collector
9. ABE BEAME—Mayor of New York
10. SID LUCKMAN—One of football's greatest quarterbacks
11. EMANUEL CELLER—Congressman

ESTIMATED PERCENTAGES OF JEWS IN VARIOUS PROFESSIONS IN AMERICA

Medicine—6.9 percent
Specialized medicine—9.2 percent
Psychiatry—14.3 percent
Dentistry—9.0 percent
Law—8.0 percent
Professors of mathematics—8.5 percent
Architecture—5.1 percent
Engineering—3.3 percent

THE EIGHTEEN LARGEST JEWISH COMMUNITIES IN THE UNITED STATES

Populations listed for cities include suburban areas.
These are estimated populations

1. New York 1,998,000
2. Los Angeles 455,000
3. Philadelphia 295,000
4. Chicago 253,000
5. Miami 225,000
6. Boston 170,000
7. Washington 160,000
8. Bergen County, New Jersey 100,000
9. Essex County, New Jersey 95,000
10. Baltimore 92,000
11. Cleveland 75,000
12. Detroit 75,000
13. San Francisco 75,000
14. Montgomery County, Maryland 70,000
15. St. Louis 60,000

16. Fort Lauderdale 60,000
17. Hollywood, Florida 55,000
18. Pittsburgh 51,000

Source: *American Jewish Yearbook,* 1980

JEWISH CONGREGATIONS IN AMERICA

	Congregations (approx.)	Members (approx.)
Union of American Hebrew Congregations (Reform)	720	1,000,000
United Synagogues of America	820	1,500,000
Union of Orthodox Jewish Congregations of America (Orthodox)	1,000	1,200,000

NINETEEN GUESTS AT LOU G. SIEGEL'S

Founded in 1918, Siegel's, at 209 West 38th Street in Manhattan, is the oldest kosher restaurant in the United States. Celebrities who have dined there include:

1. Eleanor Roosevelt
2. Mayor Fiorello La Guardia
3. George Jessel
4. Cyd Charisse
5. Tony Martin
6. Jackie Mason
7. Joel Siegel
8. Pres. Zalman Shazar
9. Ambassador Chaim Herzog

10. Eddie Cantor
11. Lord Mayor of Dublin Robert Briscoe
12. George Burns
13. Gracie Allen
14. Gov. Herbert Lehman
15. Mayor Robert Wagner
16. Gen. David Sarnoff
17. Prime Minister Golda Meir
18. Rudy Vallee
19. William Bendix

THREE JEWISH CONNECTIONS IN THE LIFE OF WYATT EARP

1. He married a Jewish dancer, Josephine Marcus, while he was sheriff of Tombstone, Arizona.
2. He was hired as sheriff of Dodge City by a Jew, councilman Adolph Gluck.
3. He is buried in a Jewish cemetery in Los Angeles.

Sources: (1) Bernard Postal and Lionel Koppman, *Guess Who's Jewish in American History;* (2) Stanley Feldstein, *The Land That I Show You;* (3) Bill O'Neal, *Encyclopedia of American Gunfighters.*

SEVEN JEWS INVOLVED IN KANSAS CITY'S HYATT REGENCY HOTEL DISASTER

On Friday, July 17, 1981, 111 people were killed and nearly 200 injured as walkways in the atrium lobby of Kansas City's Hyatt Regency Hotel collapsed during an evening tea dance. Among the members of the Kansas City Jewish community affected by the tragedy were:

1. ROBERT JONAS—Dead
2. STEPHEN HERSHMAN—Dead
3. PAUL WINETT—Dead
4. SOL KOENIGSBERG—Executive director of the Jewish Federation of Greater Kansas City. Suffered injuries, as did his wife,
5. ROSETTE KOENIGSBERG
6. STEVE MILLER—Conductor of the band playing at the hotel at the time of the disaster.
7. RICHARD BERKLEY—Mayor of Kansas City and director of much of the rescue efforts. Kansas City is the third largest city in the United States with a Jewish mayor, following New York (Ed Koch) and San Francisco (Diane Feinstein).

12.
Award Winners and General Achievements

TWENTY-NINE INVENTIONS BY JEWS

Name of the inventor follows the invention

1. The Polaroid camera—Edward Land
2. The thin-spoked wheel for bicycles—Nahum Solomon
3. The adding machine—Abraham Stern
4. The dirigible—David Schwartz
5. The traffic light—Charles Adler
6. The scale-model electric train—Joshua Lionel Cowan
7. Blue jeans—Levi Strauss
8. Valium—Leo Sternbach
9. The microphone—Emile Berliner
10. The girdle polishing machine for diamonds—Yeshaya Yarnitsky
11. Kosher soap—Israel Rokeach
   Until he began marketing a coconut oil-based soap in

1870, all commercial soap had an unkosher animal fat base.
12. The teddy bear—Morris Michtom
13. The drip irrigation technique—Simcha Blass
14. The gaslight—Abraham Schreiner
15. Stainless steel—Benno Strauss
16. Disc records—Emile Berliner
17. Sound movies—Isador Kitsee
18. Magnesium flash powder—Joshua Lionel Cowan
19. The calibrated laser power meter—Efraim Greenfield
20. Three-dimensional photography—Dennis Gabor
21. The refrigerated railroad car—Isador Kitsee
22. The telephone—Jacob Reis
    This German Jew exhibited a device which transmitted
    speech over a 300-foot wire in 1861. Bell acknowledged that
    he drew upon Reis's ideas in constructing his phone.
23. Fowl pox vaccine—Arthur Goldhaft
24. The transmission of photography by wire—Arthur Korn
25. The Kodachrome process for color photography—
    Leopold Mannes and Leopold Godowsky
26. The sealed mercury battery—Samuel Ruben
27. The hotdog bun—Abraham Levis
28. Flexi-straws—Joe Freedman
29. The Zapper (an electric-shock anti-mugger device worn on
    the wrist)—George Plotkin (and Kevin Rhodes)

THE WORLD'S FIFTY MOST IMPORTANT JEWS (1974)

1. YIGAL ALON*—Israeli politician
2. HANNAH ARENDT*—Philosopher and political scientist
3. RAYMOND ARON*—Sociologist
4. DANIEL BARENBOIM—Pianist

---

*Since deceased

5. ISAIAH BERLIN—Philosopher
6. LEONARD BERNSTEIN—Conductor
7. ELI M. BLACK*—Financier
8. ADOLPHO BLOCH—South American publisher
9. IRVING BROWN—A.F.L.-C.I.O. official
10. ARTHUR BURNS—Economist
11. RENÉ CASSIN*—President of the U.N. Commission on Human Rights
12. MARC CHAGALL—Artist
13. NOAM CHOMSKY—Linguist
14. MOSHE DAYAN*—Israeli politician
15. ISAAC DJERASSI—Developer of treatment for leukemia
16. ABBA EBAN—Israeli politician
17. ANNA FREUD*—Psychoanalyst
18. MICHEL FRIBOURG—Arranged massive U.S. sale of wheat to U.S.S.R. in 1972
19. MURRAY GELL-MANN—Physicist
20. HENRY A. GRUNWALD—Managing editor of *Time*
21. FRANCOIS JACOB—Geneticist
22. JACOB JAVITS—Senator (retired 1981)
23. HENRY A. KISSINGER—Diplomat
24. EDMUND KLEIN—Developer of a cancer treatment
25. NATHAN S. KLINE—Psychiatrist
26. BRUNO KREISKY—Austrian chancellor
27. WALTER LEVY—Oil expert
28. NORMAN MAILER—Author
29. GOLDA MEIR*—Israeli prime minister
30. ALBERT MEMSI—Sociologist
31. SOIA MENTSCHIKOFF—Lawyer
32. ANDRÉ MEYER—Investment banker
33. LOUISE NEVELSON—Sculptor

*Since deceased

34. OSCAR NIEMEYER SOARES FILHO—Architect
35. MARSCHALL NIRENBERG—Biochemist
36. HAROLD PINTER—Playwright
37. MOSHE ROSEN—Activist Chief Rabbi of Rumania
38. GUY DE ROTHSCHILD—French banker
39. VICTOR ROTHSCHILD—British banker
40. PAUL SAMUELSON—Economist
41. PINCHAS SAPIR*—Israeli politician
42. ROBERT SARNOFF—Chairman of the board of R.C.A.
43. IRVING SHAPIRO—Chairman of the board of Du Pont
44. BEVERLY SILLS—Opera star
45. ARTHUR OCHS SULZBERGER—Publisher of *The New York Times*
46. HELEN SUZMAN—Liberal South African politician
47. GEORGE WALD—Biologist
48. SIEGMUND G. WARBURG—Banker
49. JEROME B. WIESNER—President of M.I.T.
50. ISAAC WOLFSON—British businessman and philanthropist

This list reprinted, with permission, from the Winter 1974 issue of *Present Tense* magazine, Copyright© 1974 *Present Tense.*

Permit me to nominate Menachem Begin, the Israeli prime minister; Shimon Peres, the Israeli opposition leader; and Anatoly Shcharansky, the imprisoned Soviet Jewish dissident, as replacements for several of the deceased and retired individuals on the above list. Others who should be added, too, are Ed Koch, mayor of New York City; Norman Lear, the television producer; Itzhak Perlman, the violinist; Steven Spielberg, the movie producer; and Yoseph Mendlovitz, the Soviet Jewish dissident now living in Israel.

---

*Since deceased

Six *Time* "Man of the Year" Awards Shared by Jews

No Jew has ever been the sole winner of this award since its inception some sixty-odd years ago, but Jews have shared it in the following years:

1. 1950—Jews get about 3 percent of the Man of the Year award when it goes to "G.I. Joe."
2. 1956—The Hungarian freedom fighter wins the award. Some 200,000 Jews lived in Hungary at the time, about 2.5 percent of the population.
3. 1960—Of the fifteen scientists who share the award, five, Isidor Isaac Rabi, Edward Teller, Joshua Lederberg, Donald Glaser, and Emilio Segre, are Jewish.
4. 1966—Young people under 25 win the award. Again, about a 2.5 percent share for American Jews.
5. 1969—The award goes to Middle Americans. I imagine that includes some Jews.
6. 1972—A peak year. Jews take 50 percent of the award, as Richard Nixon shares it with Henry Kissinger. (Nixon is not Jewish.)

Eighty-six Jewish Nobel Prize-winners

Since its inception in 1899, over 16 percent of the prizes have been won by Jews.

World Peace

1911—Alfred Fried
1911—Tobias Michael Carel Asser

1968—René Cassin
1973—Henry Kissinger
1978—Menachem Begin

Literature

1910—Paul Johann Ludwig von Heyse
1927—Henri Bergson
1958—Boris Pasternak
1966—Shmuel Yosef Agnon
1966—Nelly Sachs
1976—Saul Bellow
1978—Isaac Bashevis Singer
1981—Elias Canetti

Physiology and Medicine

1908—Elie Metchnikoff
1908—Paul Ehrlich
1914—Robert Bárány
1922—Otto Meyerhof
1930—Karl Landsteiner
1931—Otto Warburg
1936—Otto Loewi
1944—Joseph Erlanger
1944—Herbert Spencer Gasser
1945—Ernst Boris Chain
1946—Hermann Joseph Muller
1950—Tadeus Reichstein
1952—Selman Abraham Waksman
1953—Hans Krebs
1953—Fritz Albert Lipmann
1958—Joshua Lederberg

1959—Arthur Kornberg
1964—Konrad Bloch
1965—Francois Jacob
1965—André Lwoff
1967—George Wald
1968—Marshall W. Nirenberg
1969—Salvador Luria
1970—Julius Axelrod
1970—Sir Bernard Katz
1972—Gerald Maurice Edelman
1975—David Baltimore
1975—Howard Martin Temin
1976—Baruch S. Blumberg
1977—Barbara Sussman Yalow
1980—Baruj Benacerraf

Chemistry

1905—Adolph Von Baeyer
1906—Henri Moissan
1910—Otto Wallach
1915—Richard Willstaetter
1918—Fritz Haber
1943—George Charles de Hevesy
1961—Melvin Calvin
1962—Max Ferdinand Perutz
1972—William Howard Stein
1979—Herbert Charles Brown
1980—Paul Berg
1980—Walter Gilbert
1981—Roald Hoffmann

Physics

1907—Albert Abraham Michelson

1908—Gabriel Lippmann
1921—Albert Einstein
1922—Niels Bohr
1925—James Franck
1925—Gustav Hertz
1943—Otto Stern
1944—Isidor Isaac Rabi
1952—Felix Bloch
1954—Max Born
1958—Igor Tamm
1959—Emilio Segrè
1960—Donald A. Glaser
1961—Robert Hofstadter
1962—Lev Davidovich Landau
1965—Richard Phillips Feynman
1965—Julian Schwinger
1969—Murray Gell-Mann
1971—Dennis Gabor
1973—Brian David Josephson
1975—Benjamin Mottleson
1979—Steven Weinberg
1979—Sheldon Glashow
1980—Lawrence Klein
1982—Aaron Kleeg

Economics

1970—Paul Anthony Samuelson
1971—Simon Kuznets
1972—Kenneth Joseph Arrow
1975—Leonid Kantorovich
1976—Milton Friedman

Karl Landsteiner, winner of the Nobel Prize for medicine in

1930, once filed an injunction to prevent his inclusion in *Who's Who in American Jewry*. He explained:

> It will be detrimental to me to emphasize publicly the religion of my ancestors, first as a matter of convenience, and, secondly, I want nothing in the slightest degree to cause any mental anguish, pain, or suffering to any members of my family. My son is now nineteen years old and he has no suspicion that any of his ancestors were Jewish.

FIVE JEWISH WINNERS OF THE OMEGA ACHIEVERS AWARD

On the occasion of America's bicentennial, Samsonite Corporation polled 10,000 editors, congressmen, and educators to pick the winners of the Omega Achievers Award. The award was given in sixteen categories to Americans whom the selectors felt should serve as models for the nation as it entered its third century. Five of the winners were Jewish.

1. LEVI STRAUSS—Fashion
2. BEVERLY SILLS—Performing arts
3. CARL BERNSTEIN (Together with Robert Woodward)—Journalism
4. JONAS SALK—Science and medicine
5. GEN. DAVID SARNOFF—Television/Radio

PROFESSOR ABRAHAM KAPLAN'S* LISTS OF GREATEST JEWISH CONTRIBUTIONS TO WESTERN CIVILIZATION
Jewish Contributions to Western Civilization

1. The Bible

2. The Sabbath
3. Christianity (founded by Jews and begun as a Jewish sect)
4. The Talmud
5. Kabbalah
6. The philosophy of Maimonides
7. Hasidism
8. Yiddish language and literature (Sholom Aleichem, I.L. Peretz, and others)
9. Hebrew language and literature (Judah Halevy, Chaim Nachman Bialik, S.J. Agnon, and many others)
10. The philosophy of Martin Buber

Contributions by Jews but not Specifically Judaic in Content

1. The philosophy of Spinoza
2. Socialism and communism (Karl Marx)
3. The theory of relativity (Albert Einstein)
4. Psychoanalysis (Sigmund Freud)
5. The film industry (established largely by Jews—Louis B. Mayer, Sam Goldwyn, the Warner brothers, and many others)
6. Performing artists (Jascha Heifetz, Artur Rubinstein, Vladimir Horowitz, and many others)
7. Contributions to the development of atomic energy (Enrico Fermi, Edward Teller, and others)
8. The rebirth of the State of Israel
9. The Salk vaccine and other contributions to medicine
10. Cybernetics (Norbert Weiner)

---

*Professor Abraham Kaplan is one of the leading philosophers of our day. His *The New World of Philosophy* is a campus classic.

MORDECAI RICHLER'S LIST OF THE NINE GREATEST NOVELS WRITTEN BY JEWS

1. *The Castle,* by Franz Kafka
2. *Riding with the Red Cavalry,* by Isaac Babel
3. *Seize the Day,* by Saul Bellow
4. *Mr. Sammler's Planet,* by Saul Bellow
5. *Call It Sleep,* by Henry Roth
6. *Portnoy's Complaint,* by Philip Roth
7. *The Magician of Lublin,* by Isaac Bashevis Singer
8. *Catch-22,* by Joseph Heller
9. *The Deer Park,* by Norman Mailer

SIX JEWS WHO WON THE PULITZER PRIZE FOR FICTION

1. EDNA FERBER (1925)—*So Big*
2. HERMAN WOUK (1952)—*The Caine Mutiny*
3. MACKINLAY KANTOR (1956)—*Andersonville*
4. BERNARD MALAMUD (1967)—*The Fixer*
5. SAUL BELLOW (1976)—*Humboldt's Gift*
6. NORMAN MAILER (1980)—*The Executioner's Song*

13.
Psychology

SIX JEWISH PSYCHOLOGISTS YOU WON'T FIND IN THE ENCYCLOPEDIA

1. DR. JOYCE BROTHERS—The popular TV personality and syndicated columnist first came to fame through her expertise in boxing lore on television's "$64,000 Question."
2. JACOB RODRIGUES PEREIRE (1715-80)—The first teacher of deaf mutes.
3. RABBI CHAIM LIFSHITZ—A student of Piaget, the bearded Jerusalem Talmudist is the founder of the first authentically Jewish school of psychology, combining modern psychological techniques with ancient Jewish wisdom.
4. TSIPORA KATZ—Another Israeli student of Piaget, Katz devised the only successful method of treatment for dyslexia, a mental disorder in which people of otherwise normal intelligence are incapable of learning to read.
5. RABBI ISRAEL SALANTER—Lithuania's leading rabbi in the mid-nineteenth century, Salanter discussed the subconscious in his writings half a century before Freud. He referred to it as the "dim faculties" (*kochot kehim*).

6. EUGENE SCHOENFELD—Dr. Schoenfeld worked in the late 1960s and early '70s at San Francisco's Center for Special Problems, a psychiatric clinic that specialized in the sexual and drug-related problems of the "hippie" counterculture. Under the name Dr. HIPpocrates, his medical and psychiatric column syndicated in the underground press reached a readership of millions.

Prof. Arnold Lazarus's List of the Greatest Jewish Psychologists

Dr. Arnold Lazarus, professor of psychology at Rutgers University, is one of the world's leading psychotherapists. He is the developer of the multimodal method of behavior therapy and author or co-author of *Behavior Therapy and Beyond, I Can If I Want To,* and *Multimodal Behavior Therapy.* When I asked him to compose a list of leading Jewish psychologists, he sent the following reply:

I have been giving a great deal of thought to the list of men whom I regard as the greatest Jewish psychotherapists, living or dead. In some ways, I find this an impossible request. What makes a person a "great psychotherapist"? Are we talking about clinical skills? If so, of all the therapists I have seen in action over the past 20 years, Allen Fay, M.D., a psychiatrist who practices in New York City, would be first on my list. Are we talking about people who have contributed substantially to the literature? If so, Alfred Adler, Albert Ellis, Victor Frankl, Arnold Goldstein, and Perry London would each appear on my list. I would also include people like Freud, Eric Berne, Salvador Minuchin, Lewis Wolberg, Andrew Salter, Aaron T. Beck, Jerome Singer, Leonard Ullmann, and Leonard Krasner—each for entirely different reasons. I would certainly want to see Jerry Davison and Marvin Goldfried on my list.

As you can gather from what I am saying, I am unable to come up with a definitive list that would make much general sense. Perhaps you might want to use an objective list of names. For example, in the December 1978 *American Psychologist*, Norman S. Endler, J. Philippe Rushton, and Henry L. Roediger III provided a list of the top 100 American, Canadian and British psychologists most cited in the professional literature. From their list, here are the most cited Jewish clinical psychologists:

E.H. Erikson
J.B. Rotter
E. Fromm
A. Freud
F.E. Fielder
A.A. Lazarus

Come to think of it, in examining the list of 100 names, I am not sure who is a *clinical* psychologist and who is Jewish, so I may have left some people out.

PROF. ALBERT ELLIS' LIST OF
THE GREATEST JEWISH PSYCHOTHERAPISTS

Dr. Albert Ellis, director of the Institute for Rational-Emotive Therapy, is considered the dean of American behavior therapists. His main criterion for choosing those who appear on his list was the fact that they made public contributions to the art and science of psychotherapy and had a significant following. The inclusion of a name in this list does not necessarily mean that Dr. Ellis endorses that person's viewpoint; in some cases he disagrees. Question marks indicate those psychologists whom neither Prof. Ellis nor I is certain are Jewish.

Nathan W. Ackerman
Alfred Adler
Franz Alexander
Nathan H. Azrin
Aaron T. Beck
Lauretta Bender
Eric Berne
Hippolyte Bernheim
Bruno Bettelheim
Murray Bowen (?)
Abraham A. Brill
Daniel H. Casriel
Gerald C. Davison
Rudolf Dreikurs
Albert Ellis
Paul Federn
Sandor Ferenczi
Jerome D. Frank
Viktor E. Frankl
Cyril M. Franks
Anna Freud
Sigmund Freud
Erich Fromm
Frieda Fromm-Reichmann
Haim G. Ginott
William Glasser
Marvin Goldfried
Israel Goldiamond
Harold Greenwald

Heinz Hartmann
Abraham Hoffer (?)
Arthur Janov (?)
Frederick H. Kanfer
Helen Singer Kaplan
Alan E. Kazdin
Otto Kernberg
Melanie Klein
Leonard Krasner
Ernst Kris
Arnold A. Lazarus
Richard S. Lazarus
Abraham Low (?)
Alexander Lowen
Isaac M. Marks
Abraham S. Maslow
Jules H. Masserman
Donald Meichenbaum
Walter Mischel
Jacob L. Moreno
Frederick S. Perls
Ira Progoff
S. Rachman
Sandor Rado
Otto Rank
Wilhelm Reich
Theodor Reik
John Nathaniel Rosen
Andrew Salter

Sam R. Salvson
Roy Schafer
Paul Schilder
Will Schutz
Wilhelm Stekel

Leonard P. Ullmann
Fritz Wittels (?)
Lewis R. Wolberg
Joseph Wolpe

14.
Exotic Jews

THREE INDEPENDENT JEWISH KINGDOMS
OUTSIDE ISRAEL

1. KHAZARIA—The Jewish state that existed in Crimea from the seventh through the tenth centuries C.E.
2. In 495 C.E., the Jewish leader Mar Zutra II established a small independent Jewish kingdom in Persia when the Persian King Kobad tried to impose a version of Zoroastrianism on the Jews which required the rich to share all of their property with the poor. The part of this doctrine that Jews found most objectionable was that wives fell into the category of property. Mar Zutra's army was defeated by the Persians in 501.
3. Yusuf Dhu-Nuwas, a convert to Judaism, was ruler of Himyar, a kingdom located in what is now Yemen, from about 515 to 525. He converted many of his subjects to Judaism. After killing a number of Christians who refused to abandon their faith, Dhu-Nuwas was defeated by the king of Ethiopia who attacked him at the behest of the Roman Emperor Justin I.

SIX ARGUMENTS AGAINST THE KHAZAR THEORY OF THE ORIGIN OF EASTERN EUROPEAN JEWRY

The Khazars were an Asiatic tribe who ruled the Caucasus and Crimea, from the seventh through the tenth century C.E. The story of their King Bulan's conversion to Judaism in the eighth century provided the background for Rabbi Judah Ha-Levi's *Kuzari,* one of the classics of Jewish philosophy. A number of nineteenth- and early twentieth-century historians, and, more recently, Arthur Koestler, have advanced the exotic notion that the Jews of Eastern Europe are descendants of Khazars who followed their king's lead. While it really doesn't make much difference who the ancient ancestors of East European Jewry were, neo-Nazis and anti-Zionists have eagerly accepted the Khazar theory. Its most vocal exponent has been Jamil Baroody, former Saudi ambassador to the United Nations, who has harped on the theme in his speeches before that body. Historians generally reject the theory and trace East European Jewry to medieval Germany for the following reasons:

1. While some Khazars other than the king did convert, they were generally of the small class of the nobility, hardly enough to account for the millions of Jews in Eastern Europe.
2. There exists legal correspondence dating back to the twelfth century between East European Jews and German rabbis, the nature of which indicates that the Germans were looked to as the highest legal authority. Had the Easterners but recently emigrated from Khazaria, they would be expected to look to their previous contacts in Middle East circles for their answers.

3. In Polish Silesia, thirteenth-century Jewish tombstones bear inscriptions and names similar to those common among German Jews at the time.
4. Many extant fifteenth-century documents written by Polish Jews are in German.
5. The rites and customs of East European Jews follow the Western European tradition, not those of the Jews of the Middle East who are supposed to have converted them.
6. Most convincing of all, Yiddish, the *lingua franca* of the Jews of Eastern Europe, is a German dialect.

Martin Gilbert's *The Jewish History Atlas,* published by Macmillan, traces the large-scale Jewish migrations from Germany to Eastern Europe. The book's maps also trace the preceding migrations from Mediterranean areas and France into Germany.

NINE SECTS OF BLACK HEBREWS

1. HOUSE OF ISRAEL—Headquartered in Georgetown, Guyana, not far from Jonestown, the House of Israel is headed by "Rabbi" Edward Emanuel Washington (born David Hill). The sect practices a potpourri of religious observances, some of them adopted from Judaism. "Shalom" is the standard greeting. "Jews are the most blessed people on earth and the House of Israel is the most blessed people in Guyana," says Rabbi Washington.
2. HASHABAH YISRAEL or NATION OF ISRAEL—Headed by Michael Levy, this group originated in Brooklyn and also moved to the Georgetown, Guyana, area.
3. THE BLACK HEBREW ISRAELITES—One hundred sixty-two members of this Chicago sect emigrated to Liberia in 1965

where they unsuccessfully tried to found an agricultural colony. Beginning in 1968, members of the group started moving to Israel, where most of them have since settled in the town of Dimona. The sect's leader, Ben Ami Carter, claims that the Black Hebrew Israelites are the only true Jews. They practice certain aspects of Biblical law, rejecting rabbinic law entirely.

4. THE BAYUDAYA—A group founded in the early twentieth century by the great Ugandan warrior Kakungubu who, after studying the Bible, decided to adopt Mosaic law. He circumsised his own son and named him Yuda Makabeo. Before Idi Amin's rise to power, the group numbered about a thousand and maintained ties with Israel. They were subject to persecution under Amin's rule and their numbers were decimated.

5. THE B'NEI ZAKEN—ORDER OF ANCIENT ISRAELITES—This New York sect consider themselves the only true Jews and refer to white Jews as Edomites.

6. CHURCH OF THE LIVING G—D, THE PILLAR GROUND OF TRUTH FOR ALL NATIONS—The oldest sect of American Black Hebrews, the Church of the Living G—d was founded in Chattanooga, Tennessee, in 1886 when "Prophet" S. J. Cherry had a vision in which he was informed that the true Jews are black and that whites claiming to be Jewish are frauds. The group observes certain tenets of Biblical law but continues to revere Jesus. The sect is currently headquartered in Philadelphia and headed by Prince Benjamin Cherry, son of the Prophet.

7. CHURCH OF G—D AND SAINTS IN CHRIST—Headquartered in Bellville, Virginia, this is the largest of the American sects of Black Hebrews, numbering 35,000. It was founded in 1896 by William Crowdy who claimed to have had a prophecy that

the blacks are the Ten Lost Tribes of Israel. White Jews are supposed to have gotten to be the way they are through intermarriage. The group keeps Jewish holidays and customs but continues to adhere to the divinity of Jesus.

8. THE FALASHAS—The only group of Black Hebrews considered authentic Jews by mainstream Judaism. They are an Ethiopian tribe of about 30,000. Jewish tradition has them descending from the Israelite tribe of Dan, while according to their own tradition their ancestors were Jews who accompanied the Queen of Sheba back to Africa after her visit to King Solomon. The Falashas have been subject to persecution by other Ethiopians. In recent years hundreds have emigrated to Israel.*

9. THE ROYAL ORDER OF ETHIOPIAN HEBREWS—A Harlem group which maintains, without substantiation, that they are descendants of the Falashas. The religious practices of the Ethiopian Hebrews are closer to those of normative Judaism than those of any other sect, though they have not abandoned veneration of Jesus.

---

*For a fuller treatment see Louis Rapoport's book *The Lost Jews*.

ELEVEN PEOPLES THOUGHT TO BE THE LOST TRIBES OF ISRAEL

"In the ninth year of Hoshea, the king of Assyria captured Samaria. He deported the Israelites to Assyria and settled them in Halah, at the Habor, at the River Gozan, and in the towns of Media." II Kings 17:6

The fate of the exiled Tribes of Israel is probably history's most popular unsolved mystery. Among the dozens of peoples alleged to have descended from them are the following:

1. THE COCHIN JEWS OF INDIA
2. THE DANES—From the tribe of Dan, of course.
3. THE AFGHANS
4. THE NESTORIANS OF MESOPOTAMIA
5. THE JAPANESE—An idea fostered by the Nippon-Israel Friendship League. The league was founded by Koreshige Inesuka, who converted to Judaism while serving as naval attaché to the Japanese embassy in Paris.
6. THE BURMESE
7. THE JEWS OF YEMEN
8. THE AMERICAN INDIANS—An idea shared by William Penn, Cotton Mather, Roger Williams, and Antoine Cadillac.
9. THE ARMENIANS
10. THE JEWS OF KURDISTAN
11. THE ENGLISH, WELSH, SCOTS, AND IRISH—This is the belief of the Anglo-Israelites, a group founded in the eighteenth century which still has adherents today. They also maintain that the Stone of Scone, the coronation stone of English sovereigns, is the stone upon which, the Bible relates, Jacob laid his head.

ELEVEN JEWISH TEACHERS ASSOCIATED WITH ORIENTAL SPIRITUAL DOCTRINES

The decline of traditional American values, so marked in the late 1960s, brought with it a rise in popularity of the religions and philosophies of the East, particularly among America's youth. The scores of Eastern spiritual groups that have proliferated since then cover a wide spectrum, from cults that prey on the weaknesses of the neurotic and the insecure to groups of sane and sincere seekers of truth. Some of these might be termed religions; others no more than movements to make people aware of the existence of spiritual values. Whatever their characteristics, Jews have been present in these groups in disproportionately large numbers, both at the forefront and among the rank and file. The following are some of the most prominent Jewish teachers of Eastern spiritual doctrines:

1. SAMUEL LEWIS—Known as "Sufi Sam," Lewis popularized Sufism (a form of mysticism with its roots in Islam) along the West Coast. He died in the early 1970s.
2. "WALLY ALI" (not his real name)—One of Sufi Sam's main disciples, along with Moinadin Jablonsky (I'm not sure if he's Jewish).
3. SIKANDAR (ROBERT) KOPELMAN—A disciple of Pir Valayat Khan, one of the world's leading teachers of Sufism, Kopelman is secretary-general of the Sufi Order and Pir Valayat's most important adviser.
4. DR. ARIF (STEVE) RECHTSCHAFFEN—Another student of Pir Valayat, he is the founder and director of The Abode, a community of about a hundred in New Lebanon, New York, nearly half of whom are Jewish.
5. SHAHABADIN (LONNIE) LESS—Another student of Pir Valayat, he lectures on Sufism around the country.
6. PURAN BAIR—Yet another disciple of Pir Valayat, he teaches in Boston and converted to Judaism before marrying his Jewish wife.
7. ALBERT RUDOLPH—Known as "Swami Rudrananda," he brought the doctrine of kundalini yoga to the West and founded the Rudrananda Ashram in Bloomington, Indiana. He died in a plane crash in 1973. (The New York branch of Rudrananda Ashram is run by Stuart Perrin, also a Jew.)
8. BRUCE RUBIN—A student of Rudolph, he and his wife Blanche both teach at the Rudrananda Ashram. They

celebrate Jewish holidays and are educating their son to be aware of his Jewish identity.

9. BABA RAM DASS (RICHARD ALPERT)—A former professor of psychology at Harvard, he was a colleague of Timothy Leary in his LSD days and one of the first professors ever fired from Harvard. He tells the story of his meeting with his guru in India in *Remember Be Here Now,* one of several books he has written.

10. PHILIP KAPLEAN—Roshi and director of the Zen Center in Rochester, New York. He studied Buddhist philosophy at Columbia before going to Japan to study and practice Zen Buddhism with the masters in 1953. Author of *Three Pillars of Zen* and *Zen-Dawn in the West.*

11. ZALMAN SCHACHTER—A rabbi with ordination from the Lubavitch Hasidim and the Jewish Theological Seminary and a doctorate from the Hebrew Union College, Schachter makes it his business to seek out Jews in Oriental spiritual groups and make them aware of their Jewishness. His efforts have brought a number of young people to study in Jewish schools in the United States and Israel.

Seven Jews Hailed or Self-Proclaimed as the Messiah

1. JESUS OF NAZARETH—Son of Mary, the identity of Jesus's father remains a matter of dispute. While the idea that he was the Messiah was already current during his lifetime, it is not clear whether he considered himself to be the Messiah.

2. BAR KOCHBA—Leader of the ill-fated uprising against Rome in 135 C.E., Bar Kochba was thought to be the Messiah by Rabbi Akiva, the leading religious figure of the time.

3. DAVID ALROY—He proclaimed himself the Messiah in 1160 and started an armed uprising among the Jews of Iraq. The revolt failed and Alroy was put to death.

4. SOLOMON MOLCHO—A Portuguese Marrano, Molcho was spurred on to open avowal of his Judaism by the appearance in Portugal of David Reubeni, who claimed to represent the nonexistent Jewish kingdom of Khaibar. Molcho went to Safed and immersed himself in the study of Jewish mysticism, which ultimately led to his proclaiming himself the Messiah during subsequent travels through Europe. Molcho was burnt at the stake in Mantua, Italy, in 1532, after refusing a pardon conditional upon his renunciation of Judaism.

5. SHABBETAI ZVI—Adhering to the words of his "prophet," Nathan of Gaza, millions of Jews throughout Europe, Asia, and Africa were convinced that this seventeenth-century mystic was truly the Messiah. The deep and widespread disillusionment among Jews after Shabbetai Zvi's forced conversion to Islam was among the severest crises world Jewry has ever suffered. Miguel Cardoso and Mordechai of Eisenstadt were among many who claimed to be his successor.

6. JACOB FRANK—In the generation following Shabbetai Zvi, Frank proclaimed himself the Messiah and gained a considerable following among Polish Jewry.

7. SHALOM BAR-NATAN—This self-proclaimed 31-year-old Messiah used to spend his time preaching and playing his guitar at Jerusalem's Central Bus Station. He, his wife, and a handful of followers used to live in tents in the abandoned Arab village of Lifta, on the outskirts of Jerusalem.

15.
Women

SIXTEEN JEWISH FEMINISTS

1. BETTY FRIEDAN—Author of *The Feminine Mystique* and leading figure in the National Organization for Women (N.O.W.).
2. BELLA ABZUG—Feminist former Congressperson from Manhattan.
3. ERNESTINE ROSE—Prominent nineteenth-century suffragette.
4. MAUD NATHAN—Women's suffragist and founder of the Consumers' League of New York.
5. SHULAMITH FIRESTONE—Author of *The Dialectic of Sex*.
6. ELLEN WILLIS—Noted rock critic. A 1977 *Rolling Stone* article about her encounter with Orthodox Jews in Jerusalem is probably the best piece she's ever written.
7. LOUISE WEISS—Prominent French suffragette in the first half of the twentieth century.
8-9. AVIVA CANTOR and SUSAN WEIDMAN SCHNEIDER—Editors of *Lilith*, a Jewish feminist magazine.

10. ROSA SONNENSCHEIN—Editor of the first Jewish feminist publication, *The American Jewess*, founded in 1893.
11. MARGARET SANGER—Founded the birth control movement in 1912 after a friend died of an abortion.
12. MARCIA FREEDMAN—Prominent Israeli feminist.
13. ESTHER BRONER—Author of *A Weave of Women*.
14. ELIZABETH COHEN—Women's suffragist, the only woman delegate to the 1900 Democratic Convention.
15. GLORIA STEINEM—Political activist and co-founder of *Ms.* magazine.
16. ALETTA JACOBS (1854-1929)—First female doctor in The Netherlands and a fighter for women's rights in that country. Her efforts bore fruit in 1919 when women were granted the right to vote.

SEVEN BEST-SELLING NOVELS ABOUT AMERICAN JEWISH WOMEN

1. *Marjorie Morningstar,* by Herman Wouk
2. *Rachel the Rabbi's Wife,* by Sylvia Tannenbaum
3. *Fear of Flying,* by Erica Jong
4. *Sheila Levine Is Dead and Living in New York,* by Gail Parent
5. *Goodbye Columbus,* by Philip Roth
6. *Diary of an Ex-Prom Queen,* by Alix Kates Shulman
7. *Evergreen,* by Belva Plain

FIVE FEMALE JEWISH RELIGIOUS SCHOLARS

1. Bruria, the wife of Rabbi Meir (c. 100 C.E.) is quoted a number of times in the legal literature of the tannaitic period.

2. Rashi, the great twelfth-century French rabbi, used to call on his daughters to render legal decisions when he was in poor health.

3. Rabbi Petachya of Regensburg, a medieval traveler, kept a written record of his journeys. In it he relates that the daughter of the head of the rabbinical seminary of Baghdad used to lecture yeshivah students from behind a closed door. The students would hear her voice through a window without seeing her.

4. Miriam, mother of Rabbi Solomon Luria (leading sixteenth-century Lithuanian rabbi), used to lecture at a seminary from behind an opaque screen.

5. In our own day, Nechama Leibovitz of Jerusalem's Hebrew University is recognized as one of the world's leading biblical scholars.

16.
Health

Seventeen Jewish Vegetarians

1. Isaac Bashevis Singer (Nobel Prize-winning novelist)
2. Shmuel Yosef Agnon (Nobel Prize-winning novelist)
3. Rabbi Israel Baal Shem Tov (founder of Hasidism)
4. Rabbi Abraham Isaac Kook (first Chief Rabbi of Palestine)
5. Rabbi David Rosen (Chief Rabbi of Ireland)
6. Rabbi Shlomo Goren (current Chief Ashkenazic Rabbi of Israel)
7. Isaac Leib Peretz (Yiddish author)
8. Franz Kafka (novelist)
9. Paul Schofield (actor)
10. Peter Sellers (comedian)
11. Marty Feldman (comedian)
12. Rabbi Shear Yashuv Ha-Cohen (Chief Rabbi of Haifa)
13. Zvi Berinson (retired Israeli Supreme Court Justice)
14. Yehudi Menuhin (violinist)
15. Bob Dylan (musician)
16. John the Baptist (cousin and forerunner of Jesus)

17. Jesus (The case for Jesus' vegetarianism is convincingly argued by Upton Clary Ewing in his *The Essene Christ.*)

—Thanks to Dan Arbel, Albert Kaplan, and Levi Sokolic of the Jewish Vegetarian Society

EIGHT JEWISH GENETIC DISEASES

1. TAY-SACHS DISEASE—A deficiency of the enzyme hexosaminidase, which causes the body to accumulate excess fatty substances. These then interfere with the proper functioning of the nervous system, eventually leading to death before the age of five.
2. GAUCHER'S DISEASE—Another disease characterized by an abnormal accumulation of lipids, Gaucher's disease is not always fatal. Symptoms include enlargement of the spleen and abnormal pigmentation. Eighty percent of its sufferers are Ashkenazi Jews, among them Israeli Talmudist and kabalist Adin Steinsaltz. (*Newsweek*, May 26, 1980)
3. NIEMANN-RICK DISEASE—Another fat-storage disorder which usually causes death before the age of three.
4. TORSION DYSTONIA—A nervous disorder caused by an enzyme deficiency. Dystonia victims suffer limited ability to move their limbs and sometimes total paralysis.
5. RILEY-DAY SYNDROME—A disease of the nervous system whose sufferers are incapable of feeling pain. Other symptoms are stunted growth and acute vulnerability to pneumonia.
6. GLUCOSE-G-PHOSPHATE DEHYDROGENASE DEFECT—An enzyme deficiency characterized by break-up of red blood cells upon ingestion of oxidizing chemicals such as primaquine

and fava beans. This leads to chronic jaundice and anemia. Found in male Ashkenazic Jews at a rate of 0.4 percent.

7. FAMILIAL MEDITERRANEAN FEVER—A digestive disease found mainly among Sephardic Jews, Arabs, and Armenians. It is of unknown etiology and is characterized by fever, peritonitis, joint pain, and other symptoms.

8. BLOOM'S DISEASE—A growth defect. Victims are short and deformed.

Buerger's disease, an affliction of cigarette smokers which can require the amputation of limbs, is often classified as a Jewish disease, though it really isn't. It was described by a doctor at New York's Mt. Sinai Hospital, virtually all of whose patients were Jewish, leading to the misconception.

THREE DISEASES THAT APPEAR WITH DISPROPORTIONATE INFREQUENCY AMONG JEWS

1. Cirrhosis
2. Tuberculosis
3. Cervical cancer

AFTERWORD

If you enjoyed *The Book of Jewish Lists,* you may want to help me put together another volume. Send your lists, or additions to lists in this volume, *with your sources,* to:

Ron Landau
c/o A. Kahn
85-35 117th Street
Richmond Hills, NY 11418

Any contributors whose lists are published in any follow-up edition of *The Book of Jewish Lists* will be acknowledged in the book.

INDEX

RON LANDAU is an American writer who lives in Israel. He holds degrees from the University of Detroit and rabbinical ordination from an Israeli seminary.